Ruslan and Lyudmila

Alexander Pushkin

Translated by Roger Clarke

ONEWORLD
CLASSICS

ONEWORLD CLASSICS LTD
London House
243-253 Lower Mortlake Road
Richmond
Surrey TW9 2LL
United Kingdom
www.oneworldclassics.com

First published by Hesperus Press Limited in 2005
This revised edition first published by Oneworld Classics Limited in 2009
English translation © Roger Clarke, 2005, 2009
Notes and background material © Roger Clarke, 2009
Front cover image © Getty Images

Reprinted 2010

Printed and bound in Great Britain by the MPG Books Group

ISBN: 978-1-84749-130-5

Contents

Alexander Pushkin (1799–1837)

Abram Petrovich Hannibal,
Pushkin's grandfather

Sergei Lvovich Pushkin,
Pushkin's father

Nadezhda Osipovna Pushkina,
Pushkin's mother

Natalya Nikolayevna Pushkina,
Pushkin's wife

The Imperial Lyceum in Tsarskoe Selo,
which Pushkin entered in 1811

Fragment from Pushkin's manuscript
of the ode 'Liberty'

Frontispiece of the first Russian edition
of *Ruslan and Lyudmila* (1820)

Introduction

Alexander Pushkin finished *Ruslan and Lyudmila*, the second longest of his completed poetical works, in March 1820 when still only twenty years old. Hugely successful with the public and acclaimed as a masterpiece by many of Pushkin's literary friends, it was denounced by other critics for absurdity, "low" language and some allegedly immoral passages. Pushkin himself was ashamed neither of the poem's direct and modern diction nor of the gently erotic nature of several episodes; his dedication had already made it clear that he hoped it would be read by his young female contemporaries, who –

> though furtively,
> might peep at these mischievous verses
> and feel a fluttering of love.

It is strange, then, that in more recent times *Ruslan and Lyudmila* has often been dismissed as a children's book, misprized in Russia, ignored abroad.

The fact is that, despite its fantastical plot and light-hearted style, *Ruslan and Lyudmila* was written for adults – to impress with the variety of its literary pastiche, to astonish with the freshness of its idiom, to delight with the music of its sounds and rhythms, to fascinate with the inventiveness of its narratives, to entertain with the liveliness of its descriptions and to amuse with the ebullience of its irony and humour.

Alessandro Gallenzi and I began the task of bringing this masterpiece to the attention of readers of English in the edition published by Hesperus Press in 2005, but now already out of print. For this edition the translation has been extensively revised and the commentary amplified. An appendix has been added to include the material that Pushkin cut from his first edition of 1820 when he republished the work eight years later. The purpose once again is to make *Ruslan and Lyudmila* available, as the only scholarly edition in English yet produced of this seminal work of Russian letters, as an accurate and readable English translation for those who study or enjoy Russian literature, and as an exciting story well told for those who simply like a good read.

An asterisk in the text refers the reader to a note in the Notes and Commentary section, where the notes are listed by page number.

– Roger Clarke, 2009

Ruslan and Lyudmila

ПОСВЯЩЕНИЕ

Для вас, души моей царицы,
Красавицы, для вас одних
Времен минувших небылицы,
В часы досугов золотых,
Под шепот старины болтливой,
Рукою верной я писал;
Примите ж вы мой труд игривый!
Ничьих не требуя похвал,
Счастлив уж я надеждой сладкой,
Что дева с трепетом любви   10
Посмотрит, может быть украдкой,
На песни грешные мои.

Dedication

Queens of my heart, you lovely girls,
they're meant for you and only you,
these fairy tales of times gone by.
That chatterbox called Long-ago
whispered me them, and golden hours
I've spent transcribing every word.
My work of fun, then, please accept.
I covet no one's compliments –
just cherish the delicious hope
that one of you, though furtively,   10
might peep at these mischievous verses
and feel a fluttering of love.

У лукоморья дуб зеленый;
Златая цепь на дубе том:
И днем и ночью кот ученый
Всё ходит по цепи кругом;
Идет направо – песнь заводит,
Налево – сказку говорит.

Там чудеса: там леший бродит,
Русалка на ветвях сидит;
Там на неведомых дорожках
Следы невиданных зверей;   10
Избушка там на курьих ножках
Стоит без окон, без дверей;
Там лес и дол видений полны;
Там о заре прихлынут волны
На брег песчаный и пустой,
И тридцать витязей прекрасных
Чредой из вод выходят ясных,
И с ними дядька их морской;
Там королевич мимоходом
Пленяет грозного царя;   20
Там в облаках перед народом
Через леса, через моря
Колдун несет богатыря;
Б темнице там царевна тужит,
А бурый волк ей верно служит;
Там ступа с Бабою Ягой
Идет, бредет сама собой;
Там царь Кащей над златом чахнет:
Там русский дух… там Русью пахнет!

И я там был, и мед я пил;   30
У моря видел дуб зеленый;

Prologue*

By an arc of sea a green oak stands;
to the oak a chain of gold is tied;
and at the chain's end night and day
a learnèd cat walks round and round.
Rightwards he goes, and sings a song;
leftwards, a fairy tale he tells.

There's magic! It's a wood sprite's haunt –
a *rusalka* sits among the boughs –
on footpaths no one has explored
are tracks of beasts no one has seen –   10
a hut stands there on chicken's legs,
no windows in its walls, nor doors –
unnumbered wraiths stalk wood and dale –
at dawn the ocean waves roll in
and surge across the empty sands,
while from the limpid waters strides
a troop of thirty champions,
fine men, and their sea-tutor too –
a king's son passing by that way
takes prisoner an awesome tsar –   20
up in the clouds for all to see
above the sweep of woods and waves
a wizard hauls a warrior brave –
a princess pines in prison there,
a brown-haired wolf her loyal page –
a mortar in a witch's form
moves to and fro as if alive –
frail Tsar Kashchéy wilts by his gold.
The place breathes Russia… reeks of Rus!

I was there once: I sipped some mead;   30
I saw the green oak by the sea;

Под ним сидел, и кот ученый
Свои мне сказки говорил.
Одну я помню: сказку эту
Поведаю теперь я свету…

I sat beneath it, while the cat,
that learnèd cat, told me his tales.
One of those tales I still recall,
and this I'll share now with you all…

ПЕСНЬ ПЕРВАЯ

Дела давно минувших дней,
Преданья старины глубокой.

В толпе могучих сыновей,
С друзьями, в гриднице высокой
Владимир-солнце пировал;
Меньшую дочь он выдавал
За князя храброго Руслана
И мед из тяжкого стакана
За их здоровье выпивал.
Не скоро ели предки наши,   10
Не скоро двигались кругом
Ковши, серебряные чаши
С кипящим пивом и вином.
Они веселье в сердце лили,
Шипела пена по краям,
Их важно чашники носили
И низко кланялись гостям.

Слилися речи в шум невнятный;
Жужжит гостей веселый круг;
Но вдруг раздался глас приятный   20
И звонких гуслей беглый звук;
Все смолкли, слушают Баяна:
И славит сладостный певец
Людмилу-прелесть, и Руслана,
И Лелем свитый им венец.

Но, страстью пылкой утомленный,
Не ест, не пьет Руслан влюбленный;
На друга милого глядит,
Вздыхает, сердится, горит

First Canto

A tale of the times of old!
The deeds of days of other years!**

By friends and stalwart sons attended,
Grand Prince Vladímir the Resplendent*
was feasting in his high-roofed hall.
His youngest daughter he was giving
as bride to valiant Prince Ruslán;
and from a laden jar of mead
he drank their health, and drank again.
Our forebears weren't such speedy eaters,   10
nor did the jugs and silver bowls
that held the wine and foaming ale
pass speedily along the tables.
They hissed and frothed around the brim,
dousing each inner man with cheer,
as stewards gravely bore them round,
and humbly bowed to all who drank.

  Talk mingled in a muffled hum;
the guests were buzzing merrily,
when all at once a fine voice rang   20
to a clear-toned gusli's* rippling notes.
The hall was hushed to hear Bayán:*
the sweet-tongued minstrel hymned Ruslán, and
"winsome Lyudmíla", and "the garland
the god of love had plaited for them".

  Racked by the fever of his love,
Ruslán, though, neither ate nor drank.
He gazed and gazed at his dear bride,
and groaned and fumed and burned within,

И, щипля ус от нетерпенья,   30
Считает каждые мгновенья.

   В унынье, с пасмурным челом,
За шумным, свадебным столом
Сидят три витязя младые,
Безмолвны, за ковшом пустым.
Забыты кубки круговые,
И брашна неприятны им;
Не слышат вещего Баяна;
Потупили смущенный взгляд:
То три соперника Руслана;   40
В душе несчастные таят
Любви и ненависти яд.
Один – Рогдай, воитель смелый,
Мечом раздвинувший пределы
Богатых киевских полей;
Другой – Фарлаф, крикун надменный,
В пирах никем не побежденный,
Но воин скромный средь мечей;
Последний, полный страстной думы,
Младой хазарский хан Ратмир: 50
Все трое бледны и угрюмы,
И пир веселый им не в пир.

   Вот кончен он; встают рядами,
Смешались шумными толпами,
И все глядят на молодых:
Невеста очи опустила,
Как будто сердцем приуныла,
И светел радостный жених.
Но тень объемлет всю природу,
Уж близко к полночи глухой;   60
Бояре, задремав от меду,
С поклоном убрались домой.
Жених в восторге, в упоенье:
Ласкает он в воображенье
Стыдливой девы красоту;
Но с тайным, грустным умиленьем

restively tugging his moustache 30
and counting every waiting moment.

At that same noisy wedding board
were sitting three young knights – tight-lipped,
downcast and sullen. And despite
their empty jugs, they took no heed
of loving cups that passed the rounds.
The victuals did not please them either.
To great Bayán they would not listen,
but glared disgruntled at the ground.
The three were rivals to Ruslán. 40
Frustrated, deep within they nursed
the poison of their love and loathing.
One was Rogdáy, a fearless fighter,
whose swordsmanship had broadened far
the lands that wealthy Kiev ruled.
Second, Farláf, a loud-mouthed braggart,
unchallenged champion at feasting,
but poor performer under arms.
Last was the Khazar* khan Ratmír,
intense as any young man can be. 50
All three of them looked pale and grim –
the joyous feast no feast for them.

At last it ended. Guests arose
and mingled in a noisy throng;
all eyes were on the newly-weds:
the bride was looking down, as if
inner anxieties distressed her;
Ruslán, though, radiated joy.
Outside now all was swathed in shadow;
the sombre midnight hour was nigh; 60
drowsy with mead, the boyar nobles
bowed their goodbyes and made off home.
Ruslán was overcome with longing:
already in his fantasies
he fondled shy Lyudmíla's figure;
but the Grand Prince Vladímir, stifling

Великий князь благословеньем
Дарует юную чету.

И вот невесту молодую
Ведут на брачную постель;　　　　　　　　70
Огни погасли… и ночную
Лампаду зажигает Лель.
Свершились милые надежды,
Любви готовятся дары;
Падут ревнивые одежды
На цареградские ковры…
Вы слышите ль влюбленный шепот,
И поцелуев сладкий звук,
И прерывающийся ропот
Последней робости?… Супруг　　　　　　　80
Восторги чувствует заране;
И вот они настали… Вдруг
Гром грянул, свет блеснул в тумане,
Лампада гаснет, дым бежит,
Кругом всё смерклось, всё дрожит,
И замерла душа в Руслане…
Всё смолкло. В грозной тишине
Раздался дважды голос странный,
И кто-то в дымной глубине
Взвился чернее мглы туманной…　　　　　90
И снова терем пуст и тих;
Встает испуганный жених,
С лица катится пот остылый;
Трепеща, хладною рукой
Он вопрошает мрак немой…
О горе: нет подругой милой!
Хватает воздух он пустой;
Людмилы нет во тьме густой,
Похищена безвестной силой.

Ах, если мученик любви　　　　　　　　　100
Страдает страстью безнадежно,
Хоть грустно жить, друзья мои,

a doting father's grief, insisted
on giving the young pair his blessing.

   At length the youthful bride was brought
to the broad bed she was to share;   70
torches were quenched... the Love god's image
glimmered in his nocturnal flame.
Their dreams of fondness had come true,
all that love offered now was ready.
Garments, resented and resentful,
dropped down upon Byzantine rugs...
Perhaps you hear the lovers' whispers,
the soft sweet sound their kisses make,
the final murmured protestation
of shyness, interrupted?... He   80
now feels the surge of pleasure rising;
yes, yes, it's come... Then all at once
thunder cracked, lightning gashed the gloom,
the image-lamp went out, smoke swirled,
the palace, swathed in darkness, shuddered;
Ruslán's whole being was benumbed...
A hush!... Then in the awesome stillness
there boomed out twice an eerie voice,
and someone sheathed in smoke whirled upwards,
soot-black amidst the murk and fume...   90
Once more the room was still and empty;
Ruslán rose to his feet in shock,
cold sweat now trickling down his face.
Trembling, with icy hands he probed
the darkness, but without response...
Horror – the girl he loved had gone!
Ruslán clutched at the empty air;
the shadows yielded no Lyudmíla,
a force unknown had snatched her off.

   My friends, if one of you's a martyr   100
to love and suffers hopelessly,
he'll live a wretched life, it's true;

Однако жить еще возможно.
Но после долгих, долгих лет
Обнять влюбленную подругу,
Желаний, слез, тоски предмет,
И вдруг минутную супругу
Навек утратить… о друзья,
Конечно лучше б умер я!
Однако жив Руслан несчастный.   110

Но что сказал великий князь?
Сраженный вдруг молвой ужасной,
На зятя гневом распалясь,
Его и двор он созывает:
"Где, где Людмила?" – вопрошает
С ужасным, пламенным челом.
Руслан не слышит. "Дети, други!
Я помню прежние заслуги:
О, сжальтесь вы над стариком!
Скажите, кто из вас согласен   120
Скакать за дочерью моей?
Чей подвиг будет не напрасен,
Тому – терзайся, плачь, злодей!
Не мог сберечь жены своей! –
Тому я дам ее в супруги
С полцарством прадедов моих.
Кто ж вызовется, дети, други?…"
"Я!" – молвил горестный жених.
"Я! я!" – воскликнули с Рогдаем
Фарлаф и радостный Ратмир: 130
"Сейчас коней своих седлаем;
Мы рады весь изъездить мир.
Отец наш, не продлим разлуки;
Не бойся: едем за княжной".
И с благодарностью немой
В слезах к ним простирает руки
Старик, измученный тоской.

Все четверо выходят вместе;
Руслан уныньем как убит;

14

he *will* live, though, you may be sure.
But what if after long, long years
you've now at last embraced your sweetheart –
the one you've yearned for, pined for, wept for –
then, at the moment of your union,
you lose her for ever – oh, my friends,
myself, I'd sooner die than that!
Ruslán, though, still lived on, poor chap.   110

What of the Grand Prince – what did *he* say?
Aghast at the first dreadful news,
blazing with anger at Ruslán,
he summoned him and all the court.
With face aflush and fearsome frown he
demanded, "Where's Lyudmíla? Where?!"
(Ruslán stood blankly.) "Youngsters, friends,
you've always served me well, I know –
have pity on me now I'm old!
Which of you, tell me, is prepared   120
to gallop off to find my daughter?
The one whose mission is successful –
to him (*you*'ll suffer, wretch, you'll weep
for this – couldn't protect your bride, huh!)
to that man I'll give her as wife
with half of my ancestral kingdom.
Friends, youngsters, who'll accept my challenge?"
"I will," the harassed bridegroom muttered.
"I... I will," cried exultantly
Rogdáy, Farláf, and khan Ratmír.   130
"Let's saddle up our horses now;
we'll gladly scour the world for her.
So, sire, let's not prolong our parting;
don't fear: we're off to find the princess!"
And so in speechless gratitude
the old man, tortured by his loss,
held out his arms to them, and wept.

All four of them strode off together.
Ruslán was nearly dead with chagrin;

Мысль о потерянной невесте   140
Его терзает и мертвит.
Садятся на коней ретивых;
Вдоль берегов Днепра счастливых
Летят в клубящейся пыли;
Уже скрываются вдали;
Уж всадников не видно боле…
Но долго всё еще глядит
Великий князь в пустое поле
И думой им вослед летит.

    Руслан томился молчаливо,   150
И смысл и память потеряв.
Через плечо глядя спесиво
И важно подбочась, Фарлаф,
Надувшись, ехал за Русланом.
Он говорит: "Насилу я
На волю вырвался, друзья!
Ну, скоро ль встречусь с великаном?
Уж то-то крови будет течь,
Уж то-то жертв любви ревнивой!
Повеселись, мой верный меч,   160
Повеселись, мой конь ретивый!"

    Хазарский хан, в уме своем
Уже Людмилу обнимая,
Едва не пляшет над седлом;
В нем кровь играет молодая,
Огня надежды полон взор:
То скачет он во весь опор,
То дразнит бегуна лихого,
Кружит, подъемлет на дыбы
Иль дерзко мчит на холмы снова.   170

    Рогдай угрюм, молчит – ни слова…
Страшась неведомой судьбы
И мучась ревностью напрасной,
Всех больше беспокоен он,

the very thought of his lost bride   140
tormented him and mortified him.
They leapt astride their sprightly stallions;
and off they flew along the Dnieper's*
well-favoured banks in clouds of dust.
Soon they were fading into distance;
soon they'd completely passed from sight;
but the Grand Prince still lingered long
and looked out on the empty steppe,
chasing the horsemen in his mind.

Ruslán bore his vexation mutely;   150
his wits, his memory had left him.
Behind him, smirking, rode Farláf,
who with a haughty backward glance
and with a condescending half-turn
said to the others: "I can hardly
spare the time off for this adventure!
Let's hope I'll meet the ogre soon.
There'll be such bloodshed then, my friends,
such carnage among jealous lovers!
Revel in it, my trusty sword,   160
revel in it, my lively steed!"

The Khazar khan was even then
fondling Lyudmíla in his mind;
he almost danced above the saddle;
his young blood pulsed, and in his eye
the fire of hope already blazed.
Now he would gallop briskly forward,
now he would tease the knowing horse
making him wheel and then rear up,
then off he'd dash uphill again.   170

Rogdáy was sullen, unforthcoming.
Unsure and nervous of the future
and plagued by senseless jealousy,
he was least stable of them all,

17

И часто взор его ужасный
На князя мрачно устремлен.

Соперники одной дорогой
Всё вместе едут целый день.
Днепра стал темен брег отлогий;
С востока льется ночи тень; 180
Туманы над Днепром глубоким;
Пора коням их отдохнуть.
Вот под горой путем широким
Широкий пересекся путь.
"Разъедемся, пора! – сказали, –
Безвестной вверимся судьбе."
И каждый конь, не чуя стали,
По воле путь избрал себе.

Что делаешь, Руслан несчастный,
Один в пустынной тишине? 190
Людмилу, свадьбы день ужасный,
Всё, мнится, видел ты во сне.
На брови медный шлем надвинув,
Из мощных рук узду покинув,
Ты шагом едешь меж полей,
И медленно в душе твоей
Надежда гибнет, гаснет вера.

Но вдруг пред витязем пещера;
В пещере свет. Он прямо к ней
Идет под дремлющие своды, 200
Ровесники самой природы.
Вошел с уныньем: что же зрит?
В пещере старец; ясный вид,
Спокойный взор, брада седая;
Лампада перед ним горит;
За древней книгой он сидит,
Ее внимательно читая.
"Добро пожаловать, мой сын! –
Сказал с улыбкой он Руслану. –

constantly turning on Ruslán
a glare of grim ferocity.

   The antagonists rode on together
by the same highroad all that day.
Then from the east spread night's dense shadows;
the Dnieper's sloping shore grew dim;   180
mists rose from the deep-flowing river:
the weary horses needed rest.
They saw then that beneath the hill
another highroad crossed their own.
"Let's separate – it's time," they said.
"We'll trust to fate, hold what it may."
The three each gave their mounts full rein
and let them choose which road to take.

   Alone now at the silent crossroads
Ruslán, poor chap, still hesitated.   190
His bride and that dire wedding day
seemed to him now the stuff of dreams.
He raised his brazen helmet's visor,
his strong hands let the reins go slack,
he rode on slowly through the grassland,
and, as he rode, within his heart
confidence waned and hope expired.

   Then all at once he saw a cave,
and in the cave a light. Dismounting,
Ruslán strode over to its mouth,   200
arched low with rock as old as nature.
He entered, dreading the unknown.
Within he found a hermit, agèd,
with placid face, mild eyes, grey beard;
in front of him a lamp was burning;
he sat behind an ancient book,
engrossed in reading. Looking up,
he smilingly addressed Ruslán:
"Welcome indeed, my son!" he said.

Уж двадцать лет я здесь один 210
Во мраке старой жизни вяну;
Но наконец дождался дня,
Давно предвиденного мною.
Мы вместе сведены судьбою;
Садись и выслушай меня.
Руслан, лишился ты Людмилы;
Твой твердый дух теряет силы;
Но зла промчится быстрый миг:
На время рок тебя постиг.
С надеждой, верою веселой 220
Иди на всё, не унывай;
Вперед! мечом и грудью смелой
Свой путь на полночь пробивай.

Узнай, Руслан: твой оскорбитель
Волшебник страшный Черномор,
Красавиц давний похититель,
Полнощных обладатель гор.
Еще ничей в его обитель
Не проникал доныне взор;
Но ты, злых козней истребитель, 230
В нее ты вступишь, и злодей
Погибнет от руки твоей.
Тебе сказать не должен боле:
Судьба твоих грядущих дней,
Мой сын, в твоей отныне воле".

Наш витязь старцу пал к ногам
И в радости лобзает руку.
Светлеет мир его очам,
И сердце позабыло муку.
Вновь ожил он; и вдруг опять 240
На вспыхнувшем лице кручина…
"Ясна тоски твоей причина;
Но грусть не трудно разогнать, –
Сказал старик, – тебе ужасна
Любовь седого колдуна;
Спокойся, знай: она напрасна

"For twenty dreary years, a lonely   210
and tired old man, I've languished here;
but now at last I've lived to see
the day that I foresaw far back.
Yes, we were meant to have this meeting;
sit down and hear what I've to say.
Ruslán, I know you've lost Lyudmíla,
and your resolve is faltering;
evil's brief moment, though, will pass:
it's not for long ill-luck will stalk you.
In hope, in cheerful confidence   220
face all that comes; don't be downcast.
Ride on, and use your sword, your courage
to fight your way to the far north.

    "Listen, Ruslán, the one who's wronged you
is the dread wizard Chernomór,
long-time abductor of fair women.
The Midnight Mountains are his realm;
till now no man has ever looked
upon that wizard's sanctuary;
but you're the one to vanquish evil;   230
you'll find an entry, and the villain
will meet his end at your right hand.
This is as much as I may tell you:
from now on, as each day unfolds,
the future's yours to choose, my son."

    Ruslán fell at the hermit's feet
and kissed his hand in gratitude.
The world glowed bright for him again,
his inner torment quite forgotten.
He had revived; but then once more   240
his visage flushed with deep revulsion...
"I know the cause of your distress,"
the old man said, "but I can quickly
dispel your fears. That grizzled wizard's
love for your bride is troubling you;
listen, be calm: his love is powerless,

И юной деве не страшна.
Он звезды сводит с небосклона,
Он свистнет – задрожит луна;
Но против времени закона   250
Его наука не сильна.
Ревнивый, трепетный хранитель
Замков безжалостных дверей,
Он только немощный мучитель
Прелестной пленницы своей.
Вокруг нее он молча бродит,
Клянет жестокий жребий свой…
Но, добрый витязь, день проходит,
А нужен для тебя покой".

Руслан на мягкий мох ложится   260
Пред умирающим огнем;
Он ищет позабыться сном,
Вздыхает, медленно вертится…
Напрасно! Витязь наконец:
"Не спится что-то, мой отец!
Что делать: болен я душою,
И сон не в сон, как тошно жить.
Позволь мне сердце освежить
Твоей беседою святою.
Прости мне дерзостный вопрос.   270
Откройся: кто ты, благодатный,
Судьбы наперсник непонятный?
В пустыню кто тебя занес?"

Вздохнув с улыбкою печальной,
Старик в ответ: "Любезный сын,
Уж я забыл отчизны дальной
Угрюмый край. Природный финн,
В долинах, нам одним известных,
Гоняя стадо сел окрестных,
В беспечной юности я знал   280
Одни дремучие дубравы,
Ручьи, пещеры наших скал
Да дикой бедности забавы.

there's nothing for the girl to fear.
He can bring down the stars from heaven,
he'll whistle, and the moon will tremble –
yes, but against the laws of time   250
his magic has no potency.
Zealous and fretful guard he may be
of bolted and unyielding doors,
but he's too feeble to molest
the lovely girl imprisoned there.
He just struts round her saying nothing,
or damns his fate's perversity…
But, warrior friend, the time is late,
and you must take your needful rest."

Ruslán lay down upon a bed   260
of moss before the dying fire.
He tried to lose himself in sleep,
drew heavy breaths, and tossed and turned…
to no avail. At last he said:
"Father, I just can't settle down.
What's to be done? I'm sick at heart;
sleep's no sleep when you're tired of living.
Please talk to me and let me draw
refreshment from your precious words.
Forgive me a presumptuous question.   270
You are a holy man, discerning –
strangely – the future. But who *are* you?
Who brought you to this wilderness?"

With a sad smile the old man sighed
and said in answer: "My dear son,
I'd put from mind my distant homeland –
harsh place it was. I'm Finnish-born.*
In valleys no one knew but us,
I herded local peasants' cattle;
my young days were idyllic; just   280
thick shady oak woods, streams, familiar
caverns and crags, untrammelled pastimes
of rustic life – that's all I knew.

23

Но жить в отрадной тишине
Дано не долго было мне.

Тогда близ нашего селенья,
Как милый цвет уединенья,
Жила Наина. Меж подруг
Она гремела красотою.
Однажды утренней порою   290
Свои стада на темный луг
Я гнал, волынку надувая;
Передо мной шумел поток.
Одна, красавица младая
На берегу плела венок.
Меня влекла моя судьбина…
Ах, витязь, то была Наина!
Я к ней – и пламень роковой
За дерзкий взор мне был наградой,
И я любовь узнал душой   300
С ее небесною отрадой,
С ее мучительной тоской.

Умчалась года половина;
Я с трепетом открылся ей,
Сказал: люблю тебя Наина.
Но робкой горести моей
Наина с гордостью внимала,
Лишь прелести свои любя,
И равнодушно отвечала:
'Пастух, я не люблю тебя!'   310

И всё мне дико, мрачно стало:
Родная куща, тень дубров,
Веселы игры пастухов –
Ничто тоски не утешало.
В унынье сердце сохло, вяло.
И наконец задумал я
Оставить финские поля;
Морей неверные пучины

But it was not vouchsafed me long
to enjoy the peaceful life I loved.

   "At that time near our village lived
Naína. Like a flower she was,
a rare and lovely flower. Her beauty
was matchless, stunning you like thunder.
One morning early I was driving   290
my cattle to the water meadows
still deep in shade, piping a tune.
Ahead I heard the plashing brook:
there was the gorgeous girl alone,
plaiting a garland on the bank.
'My chance!' I thought. That led me on.
Such was Naína, knight! I went
to join her; dire infatuation
was the reward for my rash glance;
love overpowered my inner feelings –   300
the uplifting ecstasy of love,
and love's excruciating pain.

   "A half a year flew quickly by;
then, trembling, I declared myself;
I said: 'I love you, dear Naína.'
To my self-conscious anguish, though,
Naína listened with disdain –
she only loved her own reflection –
and with a shrug she answered back:
'But, herdsman, I do not love you.'   310

   "To me the world turned dark and ugly:
my little house, the shady woods,
the boisterous games we herdsmen played –
none of them soothed the ache I suffered.
Within my chagrin parched me, drained me.
At length, then, I conceived a plan
to leave the Finnish countryside;
I'd sail off with a band of comrades

С дружиной братской переплыть
И бранной славой заслужить 320
Вниманье гордое Наины.
Я вызвал смелых рыбаков
Искать опасностей и злата.
Впервые тихий край отцов
Услышал бранный звук булата
И шум немирных челноков.
Я вдаль уплыл, надежды полный,
С толпой бесстрашных земляков;
Мы десять лет снега и волны
Багрили кровию врагов. 330
Молва неслась: цари чужбины
Страшились дерзости моей;
Их горделивые дружины
Бежали северных мечей.
Мы весело, мы грозно бились,
Делили дани и дары,
И с побежденными садились
За дружелюбные пиры.
Но сердце, полное Наиной,
Под шумом битвы и пиров, 340
Томилось тайною кручиной,
Искало финских берегов.
Пора домой, сказал я, други!
Повесим праздные кольчуги
Под сенью хижины родной.
Сказал – и весла зашумели;
И, страх оставя за собой,
В залив отчизны дорогой
Мы с гордой радостью влетели.

Сбылись давнишние мечты, 350
Сбылися пылкие желанья!
Минута сладкого свиданья,
И для меня блеснула ты!
К ногам красавицы надменной
Принес я меч окровавленный,

and, braving hazards, cross the seas;
and through the fame I'd win in war   320
I'd earn Naína's grudging notice.
I dared some plucky fisher-lads,
'Come, let's find danger, let's find gold!'
For the first time our quiet land
heard blacksmiths beating steel for swords
and galleys humming, rigged for war.
So, full of hope, I sailed away
with my brave fellow-countrymen;
ten years we spent discolouring
the sea and snow with blood of foes.   330
News spread around that foreign kings
were trembling at my daring exploits,
and that their arrogant battalions
were fleeing from our northern arms.
Fiercely we fought, and cheerfully;
we shared the booty and the bribes,
and, battle over, entertained
the vanquished to a friendly banquet.
For all the din of fights and feasting,
I was still haunted by Naína: 340
within I throbbed with hidden pain
and yearned to see the shores of Finland.
'Time to return, my friends,' I said.
'This armour we've no further use for –
let's hang it in our huts at home.'
I spoke – and soon the oars splashed out:
terror at last we left behind us;
and joyful, jubilant we hurried
homeward into the Finnish gulf.

   "My dreams of old were now fulfilled,   350
fulfilled now were my fervent longings!
The precious moment of reunion
had now at long last dawned for me!
I brought my sword, still stained from bloodshed,
I brought my corals, pearls and gold,

27

Кораллы, злато и жемчуг;
Пред нею, страстью упоенный,
Безмолвным роем окруженный
Ее завистливых подруг,
Стоял я пленником послушным;   360
Но дева скрылась от меня,
Примолвя с видом равнодушным:
'Герой, я не люблю тебя!'*

К чему рассказывать, мой сын,
Чего пересказать нет силы?
Ах, и теперь один, один,
Душой уснув, в дверях могилы,
Я помню горесть, и порой,
Как о минувшем мысль родится,
По бороде моей седой   370
Слеза тяжелая катится.

Но слушай: в родине моей
Между пустынных рыбарей
Наука дивная таится.
Под кровом вечной тишины,
Среди лесов, в глуши далекой
Живут седые колдуны;
К предметам мудрости высокой
Все мысли их устремлены;
Всё слышит голос их ужасный,   380
Что было и что будет вновь,
И грозной воле их подвластны
И гроб и самая любовь.

И я, любви искатель жадный,
Решился в грусти безотрадной
Наину чарами привлечь
И в гордом сердце девы хладной
Любовь волшебствами зажечь.
Спешил в объятия свободы,
В уединенный мрак лесов;   390

28

and laid them at Naína's feet,
proud, lovely girl! So there I stood,
her patient slave, choked with emotion.
Round her a bevy of her friends
were waiting, envious and mute.   360
The girl, though, melted back among them,
and murmured, shrugging as before:
'But, warrior, I do not love you.'

    "What good is it, my son, to try
to tell what I've no strength to retell?
Yes, even now, alone, alone,
benumbed at heart, by death's dim doorway,
I still recall my anguish; and,
when thoughts run backward to the past,
here down my hoary beard I feel   370
the trickle of a heavy tear.

    "But listen on: there in my homeland
among the lonely fisherfolk
there's lore mysterious and awesome.
Amid thick forests, wild, remote,
a guild of ancient sorcerers
dwells deep in the primeval stillness.
Their minds they constantly apply
to elements of highest wisdom.
Everything bows to their command –   380
what has been and what is to come.
They wield a power which others dread
over not only death but love.

    "And love's the very thing I craved for;
so, vexed and anguished, I resolved
to lure Naína with black arts
and to use witchcraft to ignite
a flame of love in that cold heart.
So from society I fled
into those dark and distant forests;   390

И там, в ученье колдунов,
Провел невидимые годы.
Настал давно желанный миг,
И тайну страшную природы
Я светлой мыслию постиг:
Узнал я силу заклинаньям.
Венец любви, венец желаньям!
Теперь, Наина, ты моя!
Победа наша, думал я.
Но в самом деле победитель   400
Был рок, упорный мой гонитель.

  В мечтах надежды молодой,
В восторге пылкого желанья,
Творю поспешно заклинанья,
Зову духов – и в тьме лесной*
Стрела промчалась громовая,
Волшебный вихорь поднял вой,
Земля вздрогнула под ногой…
И вдруг сидит передо мной
Старушка дряхлая, седая,   410
Глазами впалыми сверкая,
С горбом, с трясучей головой,
Печальной ветхости картина.
Ах, витязь, то была Наина!…
Я ужаснулся и молчал,
Глазами страшный призрак мерил,
В сомненье все еще не верил
И вдруг заплакал, закричал:
'Возможно ль! ах, Наина, ты ли!
Наина, где твоя краса?   420
Скажи, ужели небеса
Тебя так страшно изменили?
Скажи, давно ль, оставя свет,
Расстался я с душой и с милой?
Давно ли?…' – 'Ровно сорок лет, –
Был девы роковой ответ, –
Сегодня семьдесят мне било.

and there I lived for years untold
learning the lore of sorcery.
At length the longed-for moment came;
in one bright burst of inspiration
I grasped life's sombrest mysteries:
the power of magic spells I'd mastered.
'Success for love, for my ambitions!
Yes, now Naína *will* be mine.
At last I've triumphed!' – so I thought.
But in reality what triumphed   400
was my ill luck – it stalked me still.

  "Fresh hope fed my imagination,
desire inflamed my senses, and
I hastily intoned my spells;
I summoned spirits – in the darkened
forest a thunderbolt crashed down,
a hellish whirlwind howled around me,
the ground shuddered beneath my feet...
and there in front of me was sitting
an ancient hag, grey-haired and frail;   410
a glister lit her sunken eyes;
her back was hunched, her head was nodding –
sad image of decrepitude.
My warrior friend, it was Naína!
I was appalled; I couldn't speak;
I looked the awful phantom over;
I paused, mistrusting what I saw;
Then bursting into tears I cried out:
'Can it be?... Is it you, Naína?
Naína, where's your beauty gone?   420
Heaven surely hasn't smitten you
with such a monstrous transformation?
It wasn't surely *so* long past
I quit the world and left my loved one?
Was it so long?' 'Just forty years,'
came the girl's devastating answer.
'Today's my seventieth birthday.

31

Что делать, – мне пищит она, –
Толпою годы пролетели.
Прошла моя, твоя весна –   430
Мы оба постареть успели.
Но, друг, послушай: не беда
Неверной младости утрата.
Конечно, я теперь седа,
Немножко, может быть, горбата;
Не то, что в старину была,
Не так жива, не так мила;
Зато (прибавила болтунья)
Открою тайну: я колдунья!'

    И было в самом деле так.   440
Немой, недвижный перед нею,
Я совершенный был дурак
Со всей премудростью моею.

    Но вот ужасно: колдовство
Вполне свершилось по несчастью.
Мое седое божество
Ко мне пылало новой страстью.
Скривив улыбкой страшный рот,
Могильным голосом урод
Бормочет мне любви признанье.   450
Вообрази мое страданье!
Я трепетал, потупя взор;
Она сквозь кашель продолжала
Тяжелый, страстный разговор:
'Так, сердце я теперь узнала;
Я вижу, верный друг, оно
Для нежной страсти рождено;
Проснулись чувства, я сгораю,
Томлюсь желаньями любви…
Приди в объятия мои…   460
О милый, милый! умираю…'

    И между тем она, Руслан,
Мигала томными глазами;

It can't be helped,' she gibbered on,
'so many years have sped us by.
The springtime of our lives is over –   430
into old age we've both advanced.
But bear in mind, friend: youth's unstable,
the loss of it is no bad thing.
Oh yes, it's true, my hair's grown grey,
maybe I am a little hunchbacked,
not what I was in days of old,
not so vivacious, so attractive;
instead,' – she chattered on – 'I'll tell you
a secret: I'm a sorceress!'

   "And it was really as she said.   440
There was I, speechless, motionless;
an utter idiot I'd shown
myself, for all my 'highest wisdom'.

   "But worst of all – to my misfortune,
my sorcery had worked too well.
My 'goddess' of the grizzled locks
was now on fire with lust for me.
Twisting her gums into a grin,
she – ghoul-like and with graveyard voice –
kept grunting to me lovers' vows.   450
You can imagine my revulsion!
I looked down at the earth and winced,
while she, mid coughing spasms, proceeded
with her abhorrent talk of love:
'Yes, I've now learned to read my heart;
I realize now, true friend, that it
was formed for tenderness and passion;
you rouse my feelings; I'm ablaze,
quite overpowered by desire...
Oh come into my loving arms...   460
My darling, I can't live without you...'

   "And all the while, Ruslán, she kept
fluttering her eyes and simpering;

33

И между тем за мой кафтан
Держалась тощими руками;
И между тем – я обмирал,
От ужаса зажмуря очи;
И вдруг терпеть не стало мочи;
Я с криком вырвался, бежал.
Она вослед: 'О недостойный!   470
Ты возмутил мой век спокойный,
Невинной девы ясны дни!
Добился ты любви Наины,
И презираешь – вот мужчины!
Изменой дышат все они!
Увы, сама себя вини;
Он обольстил меня, несчастный!
Я отдалась любови страстной…
Изменник, изверг! о позор!
Но трепещи, девичий вор!'   480

 Так мы расстались. С этих пор
Живу в моем уединенье
С разочарованной душой;
И в мире старцу утешенье
Природа, мудрость и покой.
Уже зовет меня могила;
Но чувства прежние свои
Еще старушка не забыла
И пламя позднее любви
С досады в злобу превратила.   490
Душою черной зло любя,
Колдунья старая, конечно,
Возненавидит и тебя;
Но горе на земле не вечно."

 Наш витязь с жадностью внимал
Рассказы старца; ясны очи
Дремотой легкой не смыкал
И тихого полета ночи
В глубокой думе не слыхал.

and all the while her bony fingers
kept clutching the kaftan I wore;
and all the while – I well nigh fainted,
screwing my eyes up in disgust.
Then I could stand it all no longer;
I screamed out, broke away, and ran.
Her shrieks pursued me: 'Worthless wretch!   470
When I was young and innocent,
you spoiled my happiness and peace.
But now you've won Naína's love,
you throw it back at her. Ugh, men! –
They reek betrayal, all of them.
No, blame yourself, you stupid girl!
I let him hoodwink me, the scoundrel!
I gave way to infatuation...
Betrayer, monster! Oh, the shame!
You girl-thief, you just wait, and tremble!'   480

    "And so we parted. Since that time
I've spent my life in solitude,
and in the deepest disenchantment.
My only pleasures as a hermit
are nature, books, tranquillity.
Already death is beckoning;
but that old hag's not yet forgotten
the fancy that she took to me,
and in vexation she's transmuted
her love's belated flame to loathing.   490
Cherishing evil as she does
in her benighted soul, the witch
will surely come to hate you too.
But trouble on earth is not for ever."

    Our warrior heard the hermit's tales
with rapt attention; never once
did his clear eyes half-close with slumber,
nor, concentrating as he was,
did he discern the still night's passing.

Но день блистает лучезарный…　　　　　　　　　　500
Со вздохом витязь благодарный
Объемлет старца-колдуна;
Душа надеждою полна;
Выходит вон. Ногами стиснул
Руслан заржавшего коня,
В седле оправился, присвистнул.
"Отец мой, не оставь меня".
И скачет по пустому лугу.
Седой мудрец младому другу
Кричит вослед: "Счастливый путь!　　　　　　　510
Прости, люби свою супругу,
Советов старца не забудь!"

Then a new radiant day beamed out...   500
the grateful warrior with a sigh
embraced the hermit-sorcerer.
His heart now brimming high with hope,
Ruslán set off; he pressed his calves
into the neighing stallion's flanks,
sat himself snugly, whistled "forward!"
"Father," he called, "don't ever fail me!"
And off he leapt across the steppe.
The sage took leave of his young friend,
calling: "Success attend your travels!   510
Love your Lyudmíla still, and heed
this hermit's good advice. Godspeed!"

ПЕСНЬ ВТОРАЯ

Соперники в искусстве брани,
Не знайте мира меж собой;
Несите мрачной славе дани
И упивайтеся враждой!
Пусть мир пред вами цепенеет,
Дивяся грозным торжествам:
Никто о вас не пожалеет,
Никто не помешает вам.
Соперники другого рода,
Вы, рыцари парнасских гор,   10
Старайтесь не смешить народа
Нескромным шумом ваших ссор;
Бранитесь — только осторожно.
Но вы, соперники в любви,
Живите дружно, если можно!
Поверьте мне, друзья мои:
Кому судьбою непременной
Девичье сердце суждено,
Тот будет мил назло вселенной;
Сердиться глупо и грешно.*   20

    Когда Рогдай неукротимый,
Глухим предчувствием томимый,
Оставя спутников своих,
Пустился в край уединенный
И ехал меж пустынь лесных,
В глубоку думу погруженный —
Злой дух тревожил и смущал
Его тоскующую душу,
И витязь пасмурный шептал:
"Убью!… преграды все разрушу…   30
Руслан!… узнаешь ты меня…

Second Canto

You that compete in the art of warfare,
go fighting on among yourselves;
pay the grim fee for martial glory,
get yourselves drunk on enmity!
The rest of us may look on numbly,
dismayed at your dire victories:
but don't imagine you'll be pitied,
don't look to us to intervene.
But *your* way of competing's different,
you champions of poetry: 10
try not to have folk ridicule you
by quarrelling too noisily;
fight if you must, but with discretion.
You, though, competitors in love,
live amicably, if you can!
Believe me when I say, good friends –
once a man's won a girl's devotion,
that's that – there's nothing to be done:
no one will shake that girl's affection;
it's foolish to protest, and wrong.   20

   Rogdáy, though, was implacable.
Once parted from his knight-companions,
still vexed by vague presentiments,
he launched out into lonely country.
He cantered through deserted forests;
and, as he rode on deep in thought,
an evil spirit kept disturbing
and harassing his anguished soul;
grimacing bitterly, he muttered:
"I'll kill him... I'll let nothing stop me...   30
Ruslán!... you'll learn the man I am...

Теперь-то девица поплачет…"
И вдруг, поворотив коня,
Во весь опор назад он скачет.

В то время доблестный Фарлаф,
Всё утро сладко продремав,
Укрывшись от лучей полдневных,
У ручейка, наедине,
Для подкрепленья сил душевных,
Обедал в мирной тишине.   40
Как вдруг он видит: кто-то в поле,
Как буря, мчится на коне;
И, времени не тратя боле,
Фарлаф, покинув свой обед,
Копье, кольчугу, шлем, перчатки,
Вскочил в седло и без оглядки
Летит – а тот за ним вослед.
"Остановись, беглец бесчестный! –
Кричит Фарлафу неизвестный. –
Презренный, дай себя догнать!   50
Дай голову с тебя сорвать!"
Фарлаф, узнавши глас Рогдая,
Со страха скорчась, обмирал
И, верной смерти ожидая,
Коня еще быстрее гнал.
Так точно заяц торопливый,
Прижавши уши боязливо,
По кочкам, полем, сквозь леса
Скачками мчится ото пса.

На месте славного побега   60
Весной растопленного снега
Потоки мутные текли
И рыли влажну грудь земли.
Ко рву примчался конь ретивый,
Взмахнул хвостом и белой гривой,
Бразды стальные закусил
И через ров перескочил;
Но робкий всадник вверх ногами

Soon now I'll have your girl in tears…"
Then all at once he turned his horse
and galloped back the way he'd come.

    Farláf meanwhile had spent the morning
(valiant as ever) fast asleep.
Now, shaded from the noonday sun,
he sat alone beside a brook,
and to restore the inner man
was tranquilly consuming lunch.   40
Then suddenly he saw a rider
racing like wind across the steppe;
Farláf was not for wasting time:
he left his lunch, his coat of mail,
his lance, his helmet and his gloves,
leapt to the saddle and was off,
no backward glance. The other chased him.
"Stop!" cried the unknown man behind him,
"Runaway, stop! You shameless wretch!
Coward, just let me catch you up!   50
I'll cut that head from off your torso!"
Farláf, who recognized Rogdáy's voice,
cowered with fear and felt quite faint.
Anticipating certain death,
he drove his stallion faster still.
In just this way a harried hare,
timorously pressing back his ears,
will bound across hills, woods and grasslands,
with hunter's hound in hot pursuit.

    Now, where Farláf was taking flight   60
in such fine style, spring's melted snows
were gushing down in muddied streams
scoring the soft, damp earth with gullies.
Farláf's spry stallion neared one torrent,
tossed his white mane and flicked his tail,
clenched in his teeth the bit of steel,
and took a leap across the spate.
Our rider panicked, though, and tumbled

Свалился тяжко в грязный ров,
Земли не взвидел с небесами   70
И смерть принять уж был готов.
Рогдай к оврагу подлетает;
Жестокий меч уж занесен;
"Погибни, трус! Умри!" – вещает…
Вдруг узнает Фарлафа он;
Глядит, и руки опустились;
Досада, изумленье, гнев
В его чертах изобразились;
Скрыпя зубами, онемев,
Герой, с поникшею главою   80
Скорей отъехав ото рва,
Бесился… но едва, едва
Сам не смеялся над собою.

Тогда он встретил под горой
Старушечку чуть-чуть живую,
Горбатую, совсем седую.
Она дорожною клюкой
Ему на север указала.
"Ты там найдешь его", – сказала.
Рогдай весельем закипел   90
И к верной смерти полетел.

А наш Фарлаф? Во рву остался,
Дохнуть не смея; про себя
Он, лежа, думал: жив ли я?
Куда соперник злой девался?
Вдруг слышит прямо над собой
Старухи голос гробовой:
"Встань, молодец: всё тихо в поле;
Ты никого не встретишь боле;
Я привела тебе коня;   100
Вставай, послушайся меня".
Смущенный витязь поневоле
Ползком оставил грязный ров;
Окрестность робко озирая,

head over heels into the mud.
Earth and sky mingled in a blur, and   70
he braced himself for early death...
Rogdáy soon reached the gully's edge,
sword brandished for a brutal blow.
"Die, coward, die!" Rogdáy gave sentence...
But then he recognized Farláf;
he stared, and let his arms drop down;
his face displayed astonishment,
disgust and anger in succession.
Grinding his teeth, struck dumb with rage,
the warrior turned his eyes away   80
and swiftly rode from the ravine
in fury... though he wasn't far
from laughing at himself instead.

   Soon afterwards beneath a hill
he came across a hunch-backed hag,
hardly alive – so old and grey.
She used a crutch to help her walk and
pointed him with it to the north:
"That's where you'll find your man," she said.
At this Rogdáy seethed with delight   90
and galloped off – to death, for sure.

   Farláf remained there in the gully;
he dared not breathe, but lay there asking
himself: "Am I alive, or dead?
That vicious rival, where's he lurking?"
Then suddenly he heard above him
the ancient hag's sepulchral voice:
"Get up, young man: the coast is clear;
you won't meet anybody now;
I've brought your stallion back for you;   100
get up, and follow my instructions."
Farláf, abashed, did as she said and
crept from the mire on hands and knees.
Looking around him warily

Вздохнул и молвил оживая:
"Ну, слава богу, я здоров!"

"Поверь! – старуха продолжала, –
Людмилу мудрено сыскать;
Она далеко забежала;
Не нам с тобой ее достать.   110
Опасно разъезжать по свету;
Ты, право, будешь сам не рад.
Последуй моему совету,
Ступай тихохонько назад.
Под Киевом, в уединенье,
В своем наследственном селенье
Останься лучше без забот:
От нас Людмила не уйдет".
Сказав, исчезла. В нетерпенье
Благоразумный наш герой   120
Тотчас отправился домой,
Сердечно позабыв о славе
И даже о княжне младой;
И шум малейший по дубраве,
Полет синицы, ропот вод
Его бросали в жар и пот.

Меж тем Руслан далеко мчится;
В глуши лесов, в глуши полей
Привычной думою стремится
К Людмиле, радости своей,   130
И говорит: "Найду ли друга?
Где ты, души моей супруга?
Увижу ль я твой светлый взор?
Услышу ль нежный разговор?
Иль суждено, чтоб чародея
Ты вечной пленницей была
И, скорбной девою старея,
В темнице мрачной отцвела?
Или соперник дерзновенный
Придет?… Нет, нет, мой друг бесценный: 140

he sighed, rallied himself and said:
"Well, thank the Lord, I'm in one piece!"

   "Mark what I say!" the hag went on.
"To trace Lyudmíla won't be easy;
she's far ahead of you by now;
I can't go on with you to get her.   110
Roaming the world is dangerous;
it won't suit *you*, I'm sure of that.
So follow the advice I'll give you:
trot gently back the way you've come;
no need to fret yourself: near Kiev,
on your hereditary estate
far from the public eye, lie low.
Lyudmíla won't escape our clutches."
She spoke, and vanished. Why delay? –
Our warrior, sensible as ever,   120
made off for home immediately,
shutting his mind to thoughts of glory
and even to the young princess;
but as he journeyed through the oak woods
at the least sound – a blue tit's flutter,
a brooklet's purl – he'd flush and sweat.

   Ruslán was racing far away now.
In wildest woods, remotest moors
his thoughts would constantly return to
Lyudmíla, his one source of joy;   130
he'd say: "My darling, shall I find you?
Where are you now, my love, my bride?
I long to see your playful glance,
to hear your gentle conversation.
Or are you fated to remain
the wizard's prisoner for ever,
wilting behind dark dungeon walls,
an ageing spinster doomed to sorrow?
Or will one of my rivals dare
to come?... No, no, my best and dearest: 140

Еще при мне мой верный меч,
Еще глава не пала с плеч".

Однажды, темною порою,
По камням берегом крутым
Наш витязь ехал над рекою.
Всё утихало. Вдруг за ним
Стрелы мгновенное жужжанье,
Кольчуги звон, и крик, и ржанье,
И топот по полю глухой.
"Стой!" – грянул голос громовой.   150
Он оглянулся: в поле чистом,
Подняв копье, летит со свистом
Свирепый всадник, и грозой
Помчался князь ему навстречу.
"Ага! догнал тебя! постой! –
Кричит наездник удалой, –
Готовься, друг, на смертну сечу;
Теперь ложись средь здешних мест;
А там ищи своих невест".
Руслан вспылал, вздрогнул от гнева;   160
Он узнает сей буйный глас…

Друзья мои! а наша дева?
Оставим витязей на час;
О них опять я вспомню вскоре.
А то давно пора бы мне
Подумать о младой княжне
И об ужасном Черноморе.

Моей причудливой мечты
Наперсник иногда нескромный,
Я рассказал, как ночью темной   170
Людмилы нежной красоты
От воспаленного Руслана
Сокрылись вдруг среди тумана.
Несчастная! когда злодей,
Рукою мощною своей

this trusty sword's still here to hand,
this head's still here upon my shoulders."

   On one occasion – it was dusk –
Ruslán was riding by a river
where rocky banks dropped steeply down.
All was quite still – and then behind him
he heard an arrow's sudden whirr,
a clink of mail, a yell, a whinny,
hooves pounding on the shadowed steppe.
"Stop!" roared a threatening voice of thunder.   150
He looked around: across the heath
a furious rider raced and hollered,
levelling his lance; at once Ruslán,
whirlwind-like, wheeled and closed upon him.
The horseman, heedless, gave a cry:
"Aha! I've caught you up. Now stop there!
Prepare to fight, friend, to the death;
you'll find your bed soon hereabouts,
so make your choice of brides from *this* place!"
Trembling with wrath, Ruslán flared up;   160
that brazen voice he recognized...

   But what about the girl, my friends?
Let's leave the warriors for an hour;
I'll call them back to mind ere long.
It's now high time for me to pay
attention to the young princess
and to the dreaded Chernomór.

   Divulging, sometimes indiscreetly,
this far-fetched fantasy of mine,
I've told you how at dead of night,   170
just as Ruslán's love surged within him,
Lyudmíla's soft and shapely form
was lost to him in clouds of smoke.
Unhappy girl! The evil wizard,
his arm braced firm by strength of magic,

Тебя сорвав с постели брачной,
Взвился, как вихорь, к облакам
Сквозь тяжкий дым и воздух мрачный
И вдруг умчал к своим горам –
Ты чувств и памяти лишилась   180
И в страшном замке колдуна,
Безмолвна, трепетна, бледна,
В одно мгновенье очутилась.

  С порога хижины моей
Так видел я, средь летних дней,
Когда за курицей трусливой,
Султан курятника спесивый,
Петух мой по двору бежал
И сладострастными крылами
Уже подругу обнимал;   190
Над ними хитрыми кругами
Цыплят селенья старый вор,
Прияв губительные меры,
Носился, плавал коршун серый
И пал как молния на двор.
Взвился, летит. В когтях ужасных
Во тьму расселин безопасных
Уносит бедную злодей.
Напрасно, горестью своей
И хладным страхом пораженный,   200
Зовет любовницу петух…
Он видит лишь летучий пух,
Летучим ветром занесенный.

  До утра юная княжна
Лежала, тягостным забвеньем,
Как будто страшным сновиденьем,
Объята – наконец она
Очнулась, пламенным волненьем
И смутным ужасом полна;
Душой летит за наслажденьем,   210
Кого-то ищет с упоеньем:

had snatched her from the marriage bed;
had, like a twister, whirled her cloudwards
up through the murk and choking fumes;
and to his mountain realm had borne her.
She'd lost all sense and memory,   180
and in one moment (so it seemed)
found herself in the wizard's castle,
pale, trembling, speechless, and aghast.

   This brings to mind a sight I saw
one summer from my cottage doorway:
that haughty sultan of the henhouse,
my cockerel, had been chasing after
a timid hen across the yard;
this lady-love he was already
enfolding in his lustful wings.   190
Above them, circling craftily,
the inveterate thief of village chickens
was calculating how to kill:
the grizzled harrier glided, hovered,
then dived like lightning on the yard.
Up whirled the evil bird and off,
in vicious claws his victim bearing
into some crevice safe and dark.
My cockerel, shattered by the loss
and by sheer terror, kept on calling   200
the hen he loved, to no avail...
all that was left – one fluffy feather
blown at him by a puff of wind.

   Till dawn the young princess Lyudmíla
lay still; the oblivion that enwrapped her
weighed heavy, like a fearsome nightmare
oppressing her. But finally she
came to herself, her brain now full
of fevered fears and vague forebodings.
She craved a friend's fond reassurance   210
and groped round eagerly for someone:

"Где ж милый, – шепчет, – где супруг?"
Зовет и помертвела вдруг.
Глядит с боязнию вокруг.
Людмила, где твоя светлица?*
Лежит несчастная девица
Среди подушек пуховых,
Под гордой сенью балдахина;
Завесы, пышная перина
В кистях, в узорах дорогих;   220
Повсюду ткани парчевые;
Играют яхонты, как жар;
Кругом курильницы златые
Подъемлют ароматный пар;
Довольно… благо мне не надо
Описывать волшебный дом:
Уже давно Шехеразада
Меня предупредила в том.
Но светлый терем не отрада,
Когда не видим друга в нем.   230

Три девы, красоты чудесной,
В одежде легкой и прелестной
Княжне явились, подошли*
И поклонились до земли.
Тогда неслышными шагами
Одна поближе подошла;
Княжне воздушными перстами
Златую косу заплела
С искусством, в наши дни не новым,
И обвила венцом перловым   240
Окружность бледного чела.
За нею, скромно взор склоняя,
Потом приближилась другая;
Лазурный, пышный сарафан
Одел Людмилы стройный стан;
Покрылись кудри золотые,
И грудь, и плечи молодые
Фатой, прозрачной, как туман.

"Where *are* you, husband dear?" she whispered.
She called out, then turned deathly pale
and looked around in consternation:
this wasn't the bright room she knew!
In misery the poor girl lay,
among soft pillows stuffed with down,
a gorgeous canopy above her.
Luxurious coverlets and curtains
were sumptuously trimmed and tasselled;   220
brocaded stuffs hung everywhere;
all gleamed with jewels, as with fire;
around her, incense-bowls of gold
exhaled their aromatic vapours –
enough, though... mercifully I
need not describe the enchanted castle:
Scheherezade* has long ago
made a good job of it for me.
But splendid chambers give no joy
when void of friendly company.   230

   Then there appeared before the princess
three wonderfully lovely girls
dressed lightly, charmingly. They came
towards her and made low obeisance.
One of the three with noiseless tread
approached Lyudmíla closer still.
With fingers delicate as air she
plaited and tied her golden tresses
(a skill still in demand in our day).
She placed a coronet of pearls   240
upon Lyudmíla's pallid brow.
After her came the second girl
casting her eyes demurely downward;
she robed Lyudmíla's graceful figure
in a rich gown of lapis-blue;
around her golden locks, her breast,
her youthful shoulders then the girl
draped a long veil of hazy gauze.

Покров завистливый лобзает
Красы, достойные небес,   250
И обувь легкая сжимает
Две ножки, чудо из чудес.
Княжне последняя девица
Жемчужный пояс подает.
Меж тем незримая певица
Веселы песни ей поет.
Увы, ни камни ожерелья,
Ни сарафан, ни перлов ряд,
Ни песни лести и веселья
Ее души не веселят;   260
Напрасно зеркало рисует
Ее красы, ее наряд:
Потупя неподвижный взгляд,
Она молчит, она тоскует.

Те, кои, правду возлюбя,
На темном сердца дне читали,
Конечно знают про себя,
Что если женщина в печали
Сквозь слез, украдкой, как-нибудь,
Назло привычке и рассудку,   270
Забудет в зеркало взглянуть, –
То грустно ей уж не на шутку.

Но вот Людмила вновь одна.
Не зная, что начать, она
К окну решетчату подходит,
И взор ее печально бродит
В пространстве пасмурной дали.
Всё мертво. Снежные равнины
Коврами яркими легли;
Стоят угрюмых гор вершины   280
В однообразной белизне
И дремлют в вечной тишине;
Кругом не видно дымной кровли,
Не видно путника в снегах,

The veil clung jealously about her,
caressed her heavenly loveliness;   250
and dainty slippers sleekly squeezed
her tiny feet – a perfect fitting!
The last girl offered to Lyudmíla
a belt of glistening oyster-shell.
Meanwhile an unseen woman's voice
was singing to her cheering songs.
Unfortunately, neither gowns,
bejewelled necklets, crowns of pearl,
nor songs of simulated mirth
could lighten poor Lyudmíla's spirits.   260
In vain the proffered looking glass
displayed her beauty, her attire:
she fixed her gaze upon the floor
and kept her silence, kept her sorrow.

    Those searchers after truth who've read
the secrets of the inmost heart –
they'll privately have realized this:
that if a woman who's upset,
in spite of habit and self-interest,
can't bring herself, through tears if need be,   270
to peep into her looking glass –
she's in a sorry state indeed!

    Lyudmíla was again alone.
With no idea what first to do,
she drifted to the latticed window;
sadly she let her wandering eyes
gaze out into the far-off gloom.
There all was dead. The snowy plains
lay in great eye-wearying carpets;
and rugged mountain peaks beyond   280
rose up in unrelenting whiteness,
for ever silently asleep.
Nowhere was there a smoking chimney,
nowhere a traveller in the snow;

И звонкий рог веселой ловли
В пустынных не трубит горах;
Лишь изредка с унылым свистом
Бунтует вихорь в поле чистом
И на краю седых небес
Качает обнаженный лес.   290

   В слезах отчаянья, Людмила
От ужаса лицо закрыла.
Увы, что ждет ее теперь!
Бежит в серебряную дверь;
Она с музыкой отворилась,
И наша дева очутилась
В саду. Пленительный предел:
Прекраснее садов Армиды
И тех, которыми владел
Царь Соломон иль князь Тавриды.   300
Пред нею зыблются, шумят
Великолепные дубровы,
Аллеи пальм, и лес лавровый,
И благовонных миртов ряд,
И кедров гордые вершины,
И золотые апельсины
Зерцалом вод отражены;
Пригорки, рощи и долины
Весны огнем оживлены;
С прохладой вьется ветер майский   310
Средь очарованных полей,
И свищет соловей китайский
Во мраке трепетных ветвей;
Летят алмазные фонтаны
С веселым шумом к облакам:
Под ними блещут истуканы
И, мнится, живы; Фидий сам,
Питомец Феба и Паллады,
Любуясь ими, наконец,
Свой очарованный резец   320
Из рук бы выронил с досады.

no merry sound of a hunters' horn
resounded round the empty crags.
Just now and then a whirlwind whipped
over the plain with plaintive moan,
and forest treetops stripped of leaves
would sway against a sombre sky.   290

   Gripped by despair and dread, Lyudmíla
burst into tears and hid her face.
What awful fate now lay before her?
She ran towards a silvered door;
melodiously the door swung open,
and all at once she found herself in
a garden – a delightful place,
much lovelier than Armida's* gardens,
or those King Solomon* possessed,
or even those of Prince Potyómkin.*   300
Groves of great oak trees met her gaze
with billowing crowns of whispering leaves.
Plentiful pools of water mirrored
palms in tall rows, a copse of bay,
a line of sweetly smelling myrtles,
the topmost boughs of stately cedars,
and golden-fruited orange trees.
Hillocks and gladed dells alike
glowed in the warming rays of spring;
and cooling Maytime zephyrs softly   310
eddied across enchanted lawns.
An oriental nightingale
trilled in the shade of quivering branches;
and pattering fountains gaily spurted
a spray of diamonds to the sky:
below them glistening sculptures sparkled
and seemed alive. If Pheidias,*
protégé of Art's patron gods,*
himself had had the joy of seeing
those works, then he'd have thrown his magic   320
chisel away in self-disgust.

Дробясь о мраморны преграды,
Жемчужной, огненной дугой
Валятся, плещут водопады;
И ручейки в тени лесной
Чуть вьются сонною волной.
Приют покоя и прохлады,
Сквозь вечну зелень здесь и там
Мелькают светлые беседки;
Повсюду роз живые ветки   330
Цветут и дышат по тропам.*
Но безутешная Людмила
Идет, идет и не глядит;
Волшебства роскошь ей постыла,
Ей грустен неги светлый вид;
Куда, сама не зная, бродит,
Волшебный сад кругом обходит,
Свободу горьким дав слезам,
И взоры мрачные возводит
К неумолимым небесам.   340
Вдруг осветился взор прекрасный:
К устам она прижала перст;
Казалось, умысел ужасный
Рождался... Страшный путь отверст:
Высокий мостик над потоком
Пред ней висит на двух скалах;
В унынье тяжком и глубоком
Она подходит – и в слезах
На воды шумные взглянула,
Ударила, рыдая, в грудь,   350
В волнах решилась утонуть –
Однако в воды не прыгнула
И дале продолжала путь.*

   Моя прекрасная Людмила,
По солнцу бегая с утра,
Устала, слезы осушила,
В душе подумала: пора!
На травку села, оглянулась –

Cascades crashed down on shelves of marble,
spray from the tumbling waters forming
rainbows of radiant mother-of-pearl;
deep in the woodland shade small streams
swirled lazily, as in a dream;
and here and there through evergreens
one glimpsed a gleaming gloriette,
refuge of coolness and of calm.
At every point along the paths   330
fresh sprays of fragrant roses flowered.
Lyudmíla, though, disconsolate,
strolled on and on, and didn't look;
the magical lushness left her cold,
the lavish brilliance just depressed her.
She wandered – where, she didn't know –
and, as she roamed the enchanted garden,
yielded herself to bitter tears;
her misted eyes she raised to heaven,
but heaven returned her gaze, unmoved.   340
Then all at once her face lit up:
she pressed a finger to her lips;
it seemed as though a wild idea
was dawning... yes, a dire escape route!
Ahead, high up above a stream,
between two rocky walls a bridge hung.
Quite overwhelmed by deep despair,
she reached the bridge – and weeping still
looked down into the sounding waters;
and, as she sobbed, she struck her breast   350
and vowed to drown herself below –
but actually she didn't jump,
she just strolled on along the path.

So my ineffable Lyudmíla,
roaming since morning in the sun,
grew tired at last. She dried her tears
and thought: "It's time I took a break."
She sat down on the grass, looked round her –

И вдруг над нею сень шатра,
Шумя, с прохладой развернулась;   360
Обед роскошный перед ней;
Прибор из яркого кристалла;
И в тишине из-за ветвей
Незрима арфа заиграла.
Дивится пленная княжна,
Но втайне думает она:
"Вдали от милого, в неволе,
Зачем мне жить на свете боле?
О ты, чья гибельная страсть
Меня терзает и лелеет,   370
Мне не страшна злодея власть:
Людмила умереть умеет!
Не нужно мне твоих шатров,
Ни скучных песен, ни пиров –
Не стану есть, не буду слушать,
Умру среди твоих садов!"
Подумала – и стала кушать.

Княжна встает, и вмиг шатер,
И пышной роскоши прибор,
И звуки арфы… всё пропало;   380
По-прежнему всё тихо стало;
Людмила вновь одна в садах
Скитается из рощи в рощи;
Меж тем в лазурных небесах
Плывет луна, царица нощи,
Находит мгла со всех сторон
И тихо на холмах почила;
Княжну невольно клонит сон,
И вдруг неведомая сила
Нежней, чем вешний ветерок,   390
Ее на воздух поднимает,
Несет по воздуху в чертог
И осторожно опускает
Сквозь фимиам вечерних роз
На ложе грусти, ложе слез.

and suddenly a tent unfurled
above her head, to give cool shade;   360
a lavish lunch appeared before her,
served ready on resplendent crystal;
an unseen harp began to play
soft background music from the bushes.
The imprisoned princess was astounded,
but her unspoken thoughts were these:
"Parted from dear Ruslán, a prisoner,
why should I drag my life out more?
Villain, your lust is self-defeating,
whether you bully or cajole;   370
your power gives me no cause for terror:
I know how I can end my life!
I've no need for these tents of yours,
these boring songs, these fancy meals –
I won't taste anything, won't listen,
I'll die, yes die here in your park!"
Then thinking stopped, and eating started.

    The princess rose, and in an instant
tent, lavish food, smart crystalware,
harp music – everything was gone;   380
all was as quiet as before.
Lyudmíla once more roamed the gardens
from glade to glade in solitude.
Meanwhile on skies of deepening blue
the moon, heaven's queen, was now afloat;
all round an evening mist arose
and settled softly on the slopes.
The tired princess drooped drowsily.
At once came a mysterious force,
more gentle than a springtime zephyr,   390
lifted the girl upon the air,
wafted her airborne to her chamber,
and midst a scent of evening roses
daintily laid her on her bed –
her bed of sorrow, bed of tears.

Три девы вмиг опять явились
И вкруг нее засуетились,
Чтоб на ночь пышный снять убор;
Но их унылый, смутный взор
И принужденное молчанье   400
Являли втайне состраданье
И немощный судьбам укор.
Но поспешим: рукой их нежной
Раздета сонная княжна;
Прелестна прелестью небрежной,
В одной сорочке белоснежной
Ложится почивать она.
Со вздохом девы поклонились,
Скорей как можно удалились
И тихо притворили дверь.   410
Что ж наша пленница теперь!
Дрожит как лист, дохнуть не смеет;
Хладеют перси, взор темнеет;
Мгновенный сон от глаз бежит;
Не спит, удвоила вниманье,
Недвижно в темноту глядит…
Всё мрачно, мертвое молчанье!
Лишь сердца слышит трепетанье…
И мнится… шепчет тишина,
Идут – идут к ее постеле;   420
В подушки прячется княжна –
И вдруг… о страх!… и в самом деле
Раздался шум; озарена
Мгновенным блеском тьма ночная,
Мгновенно дверь отворена;
Безмолвно, гордо выступая,
Нагими саблями сверкая,
Арапов длинный ряд идет
Попарно, чинно, сколь возможно,
И на подушках осторожно   430
Седую бороду несет;
И входит с важностью за нею,
Подъяв величественно шею,

The three maids quickly reappeared
and bustled busily around her,
unfastening her gorgeous clothes.
Their eyes were sad, though, and concerned;
this and their strained, self-conscious silence   400
suggested secret sympathy
and helpless anger at her fate.
But to press on: their gentle hands
soon changed Lyudmíla's clothes for bed.
Clad only in a snowy nightgown,
still lovelier in her déshabille,
she lay down in the bed to sleep.
The three girls sighed, then made obeisance,
withdrew as quickly as they could,
and pulled the door to quietly.   410
Imprisoned princess – what a plight!
She trembled leaf-like, dared not breathe;
her breasts were chilled, her eyes were dimmed;
asleep one moment – then awake,
she slept no longer, all alert;
transfixed, she stared into the gloom…
everywhere darkness, deathly silence!
Her pounding heart was all she heard…
And then, it seemed, the hushed room whispered;
footsteps, yes footsteps by her bed;   420
she plunged herself beneath the pillows –
then suddenly… oh terror!… this time
there really was a noise; the door
that moment opened, and a light
that moment beamed forth through the murk.
There entered a long line of Negroes
in pairs, with sabres bared and gleaming;
they spoke no word, they stepped out stiffly,
showing what dignity they could:
on cushions they were carrying in   430
with all due care a great grey beard.
Behind it stalked in through the doorway
a self-important hunchbacked dwarf,

Горбатый карлик из дверей:
Его-то голове обритой,
Высоким колпаком покрытой,
Принадлежала борода.
Уж он приближился: тогда
Княжна с постели соскочила,
Седого карлу за колпак   440
Рукою быстрой ухватила,
Дрожащий занесла кулак
И в страхе завизжала так,
Что всех арапов оглушила.
Трепеща, скорчился бедняк,
Княжны испуганной бледнее;
Зажавши уши поскорее,
Хотел бежать, но в бороде
Запутался, упал и бьется;
Встает, упал; в такой беде   450
Арапов черный рой мятется;
Шумят, толкаются, бегут,
Хватают колдуна в охапку
И вон распутывать несут,
Оставя у Людмилы шапку.

Но что-то добрый витязь наш?
Вы помните ль нежданну встречу?
Бери свой быстрый карандаш,
Рисуй, Орловский, ночь и сечу!
При свете трепетном луны   460
Сразились витязи жестоко;
Сердца их гневом стеснены,
Уж копья брошены далеко,
Уже мечи раздроблены,
Кольчуги кровию покрыты,
Щиты трещат, в куски разбиты...
Они схватились на конях;
Взрывая к небу черный прах,
Под ними борзы кони бьются;
Борцы, недвижно сплетены,   470

tilting his head imperiously;
to this head, otherwise clean-shaven,
with a tall nightcap perched on top,
belonged the long grey beard I mentioned.
He came towards the princess; she
sat up and jumped down off the bed.
With a swift movement of her arm   440
she grabbed the grizzled dwarf's tall cap,
raised in the air a trembling fist, and
gave such a piercing shriek of terror
as to send all the Negroes deaf.
The dwarf, dismayed, recoiled and, trembling,
turned paler than the frightened princess;
he quickly clapped both hands to ears
and tried to escape; but getting tangled
in his own beard he fell and floundered,
stood, fell again... The fuss excited   450
the Negroes like a swarm of bees;
they shouted, jostled, ran about,
then seized the wizard round his middle
and bore him off to be unwound,
leaving the nightcap with Lyudmíla.

But what about our warrior-hero?
Do you recall the unlooked-for meeting?
(Orlóvsky,* take your pencil quickly,
and sketch the scene – "carnage by night"!)
By the dim moon's uncertain glimmer   460
the warriors met in savage combat.
Their hearts were gripped with fury, both.
They'd hurled their lances from a distance,
they'd smashed their swords in smithereens,
their chain mail was bedaubed with blood,
their shields were rattling, torn to shreds...
and now they grappled horse-to-horse.
Beneath them, kicking up black earth
to heaven, the horses struggled too.
Wrestling, the men, locked tight together,   470

Друг друга стиснув, остаются,
Как бы к седлу пригвождены;
Их члены злобой сведены;
Переплелись и костенеют;
По жилам быстрый огнь бежит;
На вражьей груди грудь дрожит –
И вот колеблются, слабеют –
Кому-то пасть… вдруг витязь мой,
Вскипев, железною рукой
С седла наездника срывает,   480
Подъемлет, держит над собой
И в волны с берега бросает.
"Погибни! – грозно восклицает; –
Умри, завистник злобный мой!"

Ты догадался, мой читатель,
С кем бился доблестный Руслан:
То был кровавых битв искатель,
Рогдай, надежда киевлян,
Людмилы мрачный обожатель.
Он вдоль днепровских берегов   490
Искал соперника следов;
Нашел, настиг, но прежня сила
Питомцу битвы изменила,
И Руси древний удалец
В пустыне свой нашел конец.
И слышно было, что Рогдая
Тех вод русалка молодая
На хладны перси приняла
И, жадно витязя лобзая,
На дно со смехом увлекла,   500
И долго после, ночью темной
Бродя близ тихих берегов,
Богатыря призрак огромный
Пугал пустынных рыбаков.

held one another motionless,
as though nails pinned them to the saddle.
Hatred had tensed their every muscle;
their limbs, entwined, were growing rigid;
a fire raged fiercely through their veins;
chest shuddered against hated chest.
Then they began to sway and weaken –
soon one would fall... but then Ruslán,
with a last surge of strength, unseated
the other rider from his saddle.   480
With grip of steel he held him high and
hurled him into the Dnieper's waters.
"May that be the end of you!" he yelled.
"Die for your jealousy and spite!"

My reader, you'll have surely guessed
with whom our brave Ruslán was fighting:
it was that devotee of bloodshed
Rogdáy, stout champion of Kiev,
Lyudmíla's surly worshipper.
Along the Dnieper's banks he'd searched   490
for traces of his rival's presence;
he'd come, he'd challenged, but his strength
had let the veteran fighter down;
old Russia's legendary hero
had died a lone death far from home.
A young *rusalka** of that river,
the story went, had caught Rogdáy,
had clutched him in her cold embrace,
and with a laugh and hungry kisses
had dragged the warrior to the depths.   500
Long afterwards, at dead of night,
folk said, the hero's giant spectre
haunted those silent shores again
and terrorized lone fishermen.

ПЕСНЬ ТРЕТИЯ

Напрасно вы в тени таились
Для мирных, счастливых друзей,
Стихи мои! Вы не сокрылись
От гневных зависти очей.
Уж бледный критик, ей в услугу,
Вопрос мне сделал роковой:
Зачем Русланову подругу,
Как бы на смех ее супругу,
Зову и девой и княжной?
Ты видишь, добрый мой читатель,   10
Тут злобы черную печать!
Скажи, Зоил, скажи, предатель,
Ну как и что мне отвечать?
Красней, несчастный, бог с тобою!
Красней, я спорить не хочу;
Довольный тем, что прав душою,
В смиренной кротости молчу.
Но ты поймешь меня, Климена,
Потушишь томные глаза,
Ты, жертва скучного Гимена…   20
Я вижу: тайная слеза
Падет на стих мой, сердцу внятный;
Ты покраснела, взор погас;
Вздохнула молча… вздох понятный!
Ревнивец: бойся, близок час;
Амур с Досадой своенравной
Вступили в смелый заговор,
И для главы твоей бесславной
Готов уж мстительный убор.

Уж утро хладное сияло   30
На темени полнощных гор;

Third Canto

What good was it to hide my verses
from public gaze, for kindly friends
to enjoy in peace? They've not escaped
the angry glare of jealous eyes.
Jealousy's caused one jaundiced critic
to ask me this momentous question:
why do I seem to mock Ruslán
by calling his Lyudmíla "girl"
(as though unwed) as well as "princess"?
There's no mistaking here, good reader,   10
the sombre stamp of someone's malice!
Tell me, you Zoïlus,* you turncoat,
just how and what should I reply?
You should be ashamed, you wretch – God help you! –
ashamed! But I've no wish to quarrel;
I'm satisfied I'm in the right:
good-naturedly I'll hold my peace.
But, Clymene,* you'll grasp my meaning:
poor victim of a joyless marriage,
you'll lower your beclouded eyes…   20
I picture you: a secret tear will
fall on my lines; they touch your heart –
there now, you've blushed, you've looked away,
that stifled sigh… I understand.
Mind out, you jealous husband! Time's short;
Love and Aversion please themselves;
they've formed a bold conspiracy,
and you will shortly find yourself
a laughing stock – and serve you right!*

    A chilly dawn was glistening   30
upon the polar mountain peaks;

Но в дивном замке всё молчало.
В досаде скрытой Черномор,
Без шапки, в утреннем халате,
Зевал сердито на кровати.
Вокруг брады его седой
Рабы толпились молчаливы,
И нежно гребень костяной
Расчесывал ее извивы;
Меж тем, для пользы и красы,   40
На бесконечные усы
Лились восточны ароматы,
И кудри хитрые вились;
Как вдруг, откуда ни возьмись,
В окно влетает змий крылатый;
Гремя железной чешуей,
Он в кольца быстрые согнулся
И вдруг Наиной обернулся
Пред изумленною толпой.
"Приветствую тебя, – сказала, –   50
Собрат, издавна чтимый мной!
Досель я Черномора знала
Одною громкою молвой;
Но тайный рок соединяет
Теперь нас общею враждой;
Тебе опасность угрожает,
Нависла туча над тобой;
И голос оскорбленной чести
Меня к отмщению зовет".
Со взором, полным хитрой лести,   60
Ей карла руку подает,
Вещая: "Дивная Наина!
Мне драгоценен твой союз.
Мы посрамим коварство Финна;
Но мрачных козней не боюсь:
Противник слабый мне не страшен;
Узнай чудесный жребий мой:
Сей благодатной бородой
Недаром Черномор украшен.

but in the magic castle – silence.
Hiding his chagrin Chernomór,
in dressing gown, without a nightcap,
was yawning tetchily in bed.
Around his grizzled beard the slaves
busied themselves without a word:
one with a comb of ivory
was gently teasing out the tangles;
others poured oriental oils   40
on the interminable strands
to enhance luxuriance and fragrance;
others were deftly twisting curls –
when suddenly, from out the blue,
a wingèd snake flew in the window.
With clank of iron scales the serpent
coiled itself swiftly on the floor –
and turned at once into Naína,
to the whole company's dismay.
"Colleague," she said, "my compliments: 50
you're one whom I have long esteemed.
Till now I've only been acquainted
with you through your great name; but now
a dark fate's drawing us together
against a common enemy.
I sense you're in impending peril,
a heavy cloud hangs over you;
and, as for me, the voice of injured
pride summons me to seek revenge."
Proffering his hand the crafty dwarf   60
gave an ingratiating smile
and spoke: "Incomparable Naína!
I do so prize this bond between us.
We'll thwart that calculating Finn.
But I fear no one's machinations:
a feeble foe's of no concern.
My future's magically assured:
you see this copious beard I'm blessed with –
my whiskers aren't just for display.

Доколь власов ее седых   70
Враждебный меч не перерубит,
Никто из витязей лихих,
Никто из смертных не погубит
Малейших замыслов моих;.
Моею будет век Людмила,
Руслан же гробу обречен!"
И мрачно ведьма повторила:
"Погибнет он! погибнет он!"
Потом три раза прошипела,
Три раза топнула ногой   80
И черным змием улетела.

   Блистая в ризе парчевой,
Колдун, колдуньей ободренный,
Развеселясь, решился вновь
Нести к ногам девицы пленной
Усы, покорность и любовь.
Разряжен карлик бородатый,
Опять идет в ее палаты;
Проходит длинный комнат ряд:
Княжны в них нет. Он дале, в сад,   90
В лавровый лес, к решетке сада,
Вдоль озера, вкруг водопада,
Под мостики, в беседки… нет!
Княжна ушла, пропал и след!
Кто выразит его смущенье,
И рев, и трепет исступленья?
С досады дня не взвидел он.
Раздался карлы дикий стон:
"Сюда, невольники, бегите!
Сюда, надеюсь я на вас!   100
Сейчас Людмилу мне сыщите!
Скорее, слышите ль? сейчас!
Не то – шутите вы со мною –
Всех удавлю вас бородою!"

Unless an enemy's sharp blade   70
should slice these silver tresses through,
there is no clever warrior,
no one on earth, who can frustrate
the very slightest of my schemes;
Lyudmíla will be mine for ever,
Ruslán is destined for the grave!"
The witch with menace then repeated:
"He'll die for sure! He'll die for sure!"
So saying, thrice she gave a hiss,
thrice stamped her foot, then in a trice,   80
black snake again, away she flew.

   Resplendent in brocaded robe,
the wizard, heartened by the witch,
cheered up, determining anew
to lay at his fair captive's feet
his beard, his homage, and his love.
The little dwarf, his whiskers spruced,
stalked once again to her apartments;
through the long suite of rooms he passed:
no princess. On, then, to the park –   90
to copse of bay, to garden trellis,
past waters still, round waters falling,
through bridges, in gazebos – no!
Lyudmíla'd gone, had left no trace!
Try to imagine his frustration,
his rage, his paroxysms of frenzy!
Exasperation dimmed his eyes.
His frantic howl rang round the garden:
"Slaves, here, come here, come at the run!
This way, I say! I need you here.   100
Find me Lyudmíla straight away!
Quick – do you hear? – this very instant!
Or else – if you play tricks with me – I'll
throttle the lot of you with this beard!"

Читатель, расскажу ль тебе,
Куда красавица девалась?
Всю ночь она своей судьбе
В слезах дивилась и – смеялась.
Ее пугала борода,
Но Черномор уж был известен,   110
И был смешон, а никогда
Со смехом ужас несовместен.
Навстречу утренним лучам
Постель оставила Людмила
И взор невольный обратила
К высоким, чистым зеркалам;
Невольно кудри золотые
С лилейных плеч приподняла;
Невольно волосы густые
Рукой небрежной заплела;   120
Свои вчерашние наряды
Нечаянно в углу нашла;
Вздохнув, оделась и с досады
Тихохонько плакать начала;
Однако с верного стекла,
Вздыхая, не сводила взора,
И девице пришло на ум,
В волненье своенравных дум,
Примерить шапку Черномора.
Всё тихо, никого здесь нет;   130
Никто на девушку не взглянет...
А девушке в семнадцать лет
Какая шапка не пристанет!
Рядиться никогда не лень!
Людмила шапкой завертела;
На брови, прямо, набекрень
И задом наперед надела.
И что ж? о чудо старых дней!
Людмила в зеркале пропала;
Перевернула – перед ней   140
Людмила прежняя предстала;
Назад надела – снова нет;

Reader, no doubt you'd like me now
to tell you where Lyudmíla'd hidden.
She'd pondered her predicament
all night in tears, then – had a laugh.
That beard had frightened her, for sure,
but Chernomór she now had met,   110
and found him funny. Being frightened
is incompatible with fun.
And so, to greet the morning sunbeams,
Lyudmíla got up from the bed.
She automatically glanced
towards the tall, well-polished mirrors;
she automatically flicked
gold curls from shoulders white as lilies;
she automatically twined
her locks into a casual plait.   120
Then on one side, to her surprise,
she found her clothes of yesterday.
She sighed and dressed. Again forlorn,
she started quietly to cry.
For all her sighing, though, she kept
one eye upon the loyal mirror;
and stirred to self-regarding thoughts –
girls being girls – she felt the urge to
try on the cap the wizard dropped.
The place was quiet, no one there,   130
no one to see what she might look like...
as if there were a cap that wouldn't
suit a young miss of seventeen!
Besides, to dress up's always fun!
This way and that she turned the cap;
she pulled it forwards, straight, askew,
and then she tried it front to back...
What now? – Was this a fairy tale?
Lyudmíla'd vanished from the mirror.
She turned it frontwards – there she was,   140
the old Lyudmíla, standing there;
she wore it backwards – gone again!

Сняла – и в зеркале! "Прекрасно!
Добро, колдун, добро, мой свет!
Теперь мне здесь уж безопасно;
Теперь избавлюсь от хлопот!"
И шапку старого злодея
Княжна, от радости краснея,
Надела задом наперед.

Но возвратимся же к герою.   150
Не стыдно ль заниматься нам
Так долго шапкой, бородою,
Руслана поруча судьбам?
Свершив с Рогдаем бой жестокий,
Проехал он дремучий лес;
Пред ним открылся дол широкий
При блеске утренних небес.
Трепещет витязь поневоле:
Он видит старой битвы поле.
Вдали всё пусто; здесь и там   160
Желтеют кости; по холмам
Разбросаны колчаны, латы;
Где сбруя, где заржавый щит;
В костях руки здесь меч лежит;
Травой оброс там шлем косматый,
И старый череп тлеет в нем;
Богатыря там остов целый
С его поверженным конем
Лежит недвижный; копья, стрелы
В сырую землю вонзены,   170
И мирный плющ их обвивает…
Ничто безмолвной тишины
Пустыни сей не возмущает,
И солнце с ясной вышины
Долину смерти озаряет.

Со вздохом витязь вкруг себя
Взирает грустными очами.
"О поле, поле, кто тебя

She took it off – back in the glass!
"Oh, splendid! Right then, wizard dear!
I'm safe from every danger now;
now I'll get out of any scrape!"
Lyudmíla flushed with sheer delight,
and the old villain's magic cap
she pulled on firmly front to back.

We must revert, though, to our hero.　　　　150
It's rather shameful that we've been
concerned so long with caps and beards, and
have left Ruslán to providence.
His fierce fight with Rogdáy once finished,
he'd set off through the tanglewood;
then, as the skies first glowed with dawn,
a sweeping dale spread out before him.
Despite himself the warrior shuddered:
this was an ancient battle ground,
all now deserted: here and there lay　　　　160
yellowing bones; along the slopes
quivers were strewn, and smashed cuirasses,
horse harnesses, corroded shields;
a skeletal hand still gripped its sword;
grass overgrew a bearskin helmet;
within, a skull was rotting still;
one champion's bony frame, entire,
lay motionless beside his stallion
fallen beneath him; lances, arrows
stuck from the damp earth where they'd dropped,　　　　170
entwined now peaceably with ivy...
No voice, no sound at all, disturbed
the calm of that deserted place,
while from a lucent sky the sun now
flooded that vale of death with light.

Ruslán looked round him, heaved a sigh
and mused, with sorrow in his eyes:
"This battlefield – who can have strewn it

Усеял мертвыми костями?
Чей борзый конь тебя топтал   180
В последний час кровавой битвы?
Кто на тебе со славой пал?
Чьи небо слышало молитвы?
Зачем же, поле, смолкло ты
И поросло травой забвенья?…
Времен от вечной темноты,
Быть может, нет и мне спасенья!
Быть может, на холме немом
Поставят тихий гроб Русланов,
И струны громкие Баянов   190
Не будут говорить о нем!"

Но вскоре вспомнил витязь мой,
Что добрый меч герою нужен
И даже панцирь; а герой
С последней битвы безоружен.
Обходит поле он вокруг;
В кустах, среди костей забвенных,
В громаде тлеющих кольчуг,
Мечей и шлемов раздробленных
Себе доспехов ищет он.   200
Проснулись гул и степь немая,
Поднялся в поле треск и звон;
Он поднял щит, не выбирая,
Нашел и шлем и звонкий рог;
Но лишь меча сыскать не мог.
Долину брани объезжая,
Он видит множество мечей,
Но все легки да слишком малы,
А князь красавец был не вялый,
Не то, что витязь наших дней.   210
Чтоб чем-нибудь играть от скуки,
Копье стальное взял он в руки,
Кольчугу он надел на грудь
И далее пустился в путь.

with all these bones of fallen men?
Whose stallion galloped here triumphant   180
in bloody combat's final hour?
Who died with honour on this field?
Whose prayers reached Heaven's listening ear?
Why has it held its story secret,
grassed over by oblivion?...
Maybe I too shall fall a victim
of history's forgetfulness.
Maybe upon some nameless slope
they'll build Ruslán an unnamed tomb,
and minstrels like Bayán* will never   190
celebrate me in verse or song!"

   But soon Ruslán recalled to mind that
a warrior needs a trusty sword,
and armour too – this warrior, though,
had lost the lot in his last fight.
He roamed around the field of battle.
In undergrowth, among the bones
of unknown men, amid the heaps
of mouldering mail, smashed helms and swords
he searched for a full set of gear.   200
The silent valley woke, resounding
with rustle, rattle, crunch and clang;
he took a shield, the first he came to,
he took a helmet and a horn –
only a sword he couldn't find.
A multitude of swords he saw
as he rode round the vale of combat,
but they were all too light and small;
this prince was no effete good-looker –
unlike some army men today!   210
Ruslán, to have a toy to play with
when bored, picked up a lance of steel,
he fastened chain-mail armour round him,
and then proceeded on his way.

Уж побледнел закат румяный
Над усыпленною землей;
Дымятся синие туманы,
И всходит месяц золотой;
Померкла степь. Тропою темной
Задумчив едет наш Руслан   220
И видит; сквозь ночной туман
Вдали чернеет холм огромный,
И что-то страшное храпит.
Он ближе к холму, ближе – слышит:
Чудесный холм как будто дышит.
Руслан внимает и глядит
Бестрепетно, с покойным духом;
Но, шевеля пугливым ухом,
Конь упирается, дрожит,
Трясет упрямой головою,   230
И грива дыбом поднялась.
Вдруг холм, безоблачной луною
В тумане бледно озарясь,
Яснеет; смотрит храбрый князь –
И чудо видит пред собою.
Найду ли краски и слова?
Пред ним живая голова.
Огромны очи сном объяты;
Храпит, качая шлем пернатый,
И перья в томной высоте,   240
Как тени, ходят, развеваясь.
В своей ужасной красоте
Над мрачной степью возвышаясь,
Безмолвием окружена,
Пустыни сторож безымянный,
Руслану предстоит она
Громадой грозной и туманной.
В недоуменье хочет он
Таинственный разрушить сон.
Вблизи осматривая диво,   250
Объехал головы кругом
И стал пред носом молчаливо;

A sunset sky of pink was paling
above an earth that soon would sleep;
blue bands of fog were drifting smoke-like;
up rose a moon of glimmering gold;
the steppe grew dim. Ruslán was riding
along a dark path, deep in thought.   220
Then far off through the night-time mist
he saw a great hill looming black
and heard a fearsome sound of snoring.
The nearer he approached, it seemed
the hill itself drew breath – absurd!
Ruslán kept listening, peering forwards;
he didn't flinch, remained composed;
the horse, though, twitched his ears in terror,
shuddered, struggled against the reins,
and obstinately tossed his head –   230
so scared, his mane stood up on end.
Just then the moon, from out the clouds,
shed through the mist a pallid lustre
upon the hill: our valiant prince
stared – at a sight beyond belief!
How to describe by word or palette?
Before him was a living Head,
the enormous eyes shut tight in sleep;
snores rocked its helmet, feather-plumed;
the feathers high up in the gloom   240
were waving to and fro like shadows.
Majestic in its awesomeness,
it loomed above the darkened steppe
amid the encircling silence, nameless
sentinel of that wilderness.
Massive and menacing in the mist,
the Head barred Prince Ruslán's route northwards.
Nonplussed, the prince was of a mind
to awaken the mysterious monster.
Inspecting it now near at hand,   250
he started riding round the Head.
Stopping in silence near the nose he

Щекотит ноздри копием,
И, сморщась, голова зевнула,
Глаза открыла и чихнула…
Поднялся вихорь, степь дрогнула,
Взвилася пыль; с ресниц, с усов,
С бровей слетела стая сов;
Проснулись рощи молчаливы,
Чихнуло эхо – конь ретивый   260
Заржал, запрыгал, отлетел,
Едва сам витязь усидел,
И вслед раздался голос шумный:
"Куда ты, витязь неразумный?
Ступай назад, я не шучу!
Как раз нахала проглочу!"
Руслан с презреньем оглянулся,
Браздами удержал коня
И с гордым видом усмехнулся.
"Чего ты хочешь от меня? –   270
Нахмурясь, голова вскричала. –
Вот гостя мне судьба послала!
Послушай, убирайся прочь
Я спать хочу, теперь уж ночь,
Прощай!"Но витязь знаменитый,
Услыша грубые слова,
Воскликнул с важностью сердитой:
"Молчи, пустая голова!
Слыхал я истину, бывало:
Хоть лоб широк, да мозгу мало!   280
Я еду, еду, не свищу,
А как наеду, не спущу!"

Тогда, от ярости немея,
Стесненной злобой пламенея,
Надулась голова; как жар,
Кровавы очи засверкали;
Напенясь, губы задрожали,
Из уст, ушей поднялся пар –
И вдруг она, что была мочи,

tickled its nostrils with his lance.
The Head screwed up its face, it yawned,
it opened wide its eyes, then sneezed...
A tempest struck; the grasslands heaved;
dust swirled; up from its eyelids, ears
and eyebrows flew a flock of owls.
The silent woods awakened too.
The sneeze came echoing back – the horse,   260
on edge, neighed, reared, and galloped off;
Ruslán could scarcely keep the saddle.
Behind him boomed a deafening voice:
"What brings you this way, foolish knight?
Take yourself homewards! I'm not joking.
I'll gobble up anyone who goads me."
Ruslán turned backwards in disdain,
reining his frightened horse in firmly,
and mocked the Head defiantly.
The Head frowned, crying out again: 270
"What is it that you want from me?
I don't need any visitor.
So listen, clear off out of here!
I want to sleep; it's night-time now.
Goodbye!" But our egregious knight,
hearing the Head's ungracious words,
shouted back angrily and sternly:
"Quiet, you head-and-nothing-more!
It was the truth they used to tell me:
'The biggest head, the smallest brain!'   280
'I'll ride and ride and not ask leave,
and if I strike you I'll not grieve!'"*

    At that, the Head, struck dumb with rage
and seething inwardly with spite,
took a deep breath; its bloodshot eyes
flared up like red-hot furnaces;
its lips began to foam and tremble;
steam issued from its mouth and ears –
then suddenly, with all its might,

Навстречу князю стала дуть;   290
Напрасно конь, зажмуря очи,
Склонив главу, натужа грудь,
Сквозь вихорь, дождь и сумрак ночи
Неверный продолжает путь;
Объятый страхом, ослепленный,
Он мчится вновь, изнеможенный,
Далече в поле отдохнуть.
Вновь обратиться витязь хочет –
Вновь отражен, надежды нет!
А голова ему вослед,   300
Как сумасшедшая, хохочет,
Гремит: "Ай, витязь! ай, герой!
Куда ты? тише, тише, стой!
Эй, витязь, шею сломишь даром;
Не трусь, наездник, и меня
Порадуй хоть одним ударом,
Пока не заморил коня".
И между тем она героя
Дразнила страшным языком.
Руслан, досаду в сердце кроя,   310
Грозит ей молча копием,
Трясет его рукой свободной,
И, задрожав, булат холодный
Вонзился в дерзостный язык.
И кровь из бешеного зева
Рекою побежала вмиг.
От удивленья, боли, гнева,
В минуту дерзости лишась,
На князя голова глядела,
Железо грызла и бледнела,   320
В спокойном духе горячась,
Так иногда средь нашей сцены
Плохой питомец Мельпомены,
Внезапным свистом оглушен,
Уж ничего не видит он,
Бледнеет, ролю забывает,
Дрожит, поникнув головой,

it started blowing at Ruslán. 290
The horse tried screwing up his eyes,
dropping his head, bracing his chest,
and forcing his uncertain way
through wind and rain and dark of night –
to no avail: blinded, unnerved,
exhausted, he dashed off again
to get his breath back in the open.
Ruslán strove to advance once more,
once more was beaten back, frustrated.
And still the Head behind him there 300
kept chortling like a maniac
and roaring: "Hey, you knight, you champion,
where now? Take it more gently; stop!
Whoa, knight, don't break your neck for nothing.
Don't be shy, horseman; do a favour –
give me a jab, just give me one,
before you ride your mount to death."
Meantime it taunted Prince Ruslán
by putting out its horrid tongue.
Ruslán, dissembling his disgust, 310
menaced it mutely with his lance,
then with his free hand made a thrust:
the cold steel, quivering, plunged itself
into that tongue that dared to taunt.
Out of the maddened mouth there gushed
immediately a stream of blood.
Losing its brashness for a moment
from indignation, shock and pain,
the Head just stared back at Ruslán,
gnawed at the steel and turned quite white. 320
It can be like that on the stage:
sometimes a mediocre actor,
striving to stir himself to passion,
is put off by a sudden catcall;
the house goes blank; he cannot see,
turns white, and quite forgets his part,
he starts to tremble, drops his head,

И, заикаясь, умолкает
Перед насмешливой толпой.
Счастливым пользуясь мгновеньем, 330
К объятой голове смущеньем,
Как ястреб, богатырь летит
С подъятой, грозною десницей
И в щеку тяжкой рукавицей
С размаха голову разит;
И степь ударом огласилась;
Кругом росистая трава
Кровавой пеной обагрилась,
И, зашатавшись, голова
Перевернулась, покатилась, 340
И шлем чугунный застучал.
Тогда на месте опустелом
Меч богатырский засверкал.
Наш витязь в трепете веселом
Его схватил и к голове
По окровавленной траве
Бежит с намереньем жестоким
Ей нос и уши обрубить;
Уже Руслан готов разить,
Уже взмахнул мечом широким – 350
Вдруг, изумленный, внемлет он
Главы молящей жалкий стон…
И тихо меч он опускает,
В нем гнев свирепый умирает,
И мщенье бурное падет
В душе, моленьем усмиренной:
Так на долине тает лед.
Лучом полудня пораженный.

 "Ты вразумил меня, герой, –
Со вздохом голова сказала, – 360
Твоя десница доказала,
Что я виновен пред тобой;
Отныне я тебе послушен;
Но, витязь, будь великодушен!

84

stammers away, and then dries up,
to everyone's hilarity.
The Head was disconcerted likewise.   330
Ruslán, though, used the moment well:
his right hand lifted high in menace,
he dived upon it like a hawk,
and with his heavy glove of mail
he gave its cheek a powerful punch.
The steppe resounded to the blow;
and all around the dewy grass
turned scarlet in a spray of blood.
The Head began to reel and totter,
then toppled, rolled aside, its helmet   340
of iron clattering on the ground.
Where it had stood, Ruslán saw gleaming
a sword to suit a warrior-prince.
Trembling with joy at what he'd found
Ruslán took hold of it and ran
across the blood-bespattered steppe-grass
towards the Head, his cruel purpose
being to lop off nose and ears.
He was already poised to strike,
already brandishing the blade –   350
but then, to his dismay, he heard
a piteous groan: the Head was pleading…
Slowly Ruslán unclenched the sword:
his savage anger now abating,
the violent lust for vengeance ebbed, and
he yielded to the Head's appeal –
just so does ice melt in the valley
when caught at midday by the sun.

The Head addressed him with a sigh:
"You've brought me to my senses, warrior;   360
that blow from your right hand has shown me
that I am in the wrong, not you.
I'll do from now on what you say;
but, knight, be generous to me –

Достоин плача жребий мой.
И я был витязь удалой!
В кровавых битвах супостата
Себе я равного не зрел;
Счастлив, когда бы не имел
Соперником меньшого брата! 370
Коварный, злобный Черномор,
Ты, ты всех бед моих виною!
Семейства нашего позор,
Рожденный карлой, с бородою,
Мой дивный рост от юных дней
Не мог он без досады видеть
И стал за то в душе своей
Меня, жестокий, ненавидеть.
Я был всегда немного прост,
Хотя высок; а сей несчастный, 380
Имея самый глупый рост,
Умен как бес – и зол ужасно.
Притом же, знай, к моей беде,
В его чудесной бороде
Таится сила роковая,
И, всё на свете презирая,
Доколе борода цела –
Изменник не страшится зла.
Вот он однажды с видом дружбы
“Послушай, – хитро мне сказал, – 390
Не откажись от важной службы:
Я в черных книгах отыскал,
Что за восточными горами,
На тихих моря берегах,
В глухом подвале, под замками
Хранится меч – и что же? страх!
Я разобрал во тьме волшебной,
Что волею судьбы враждебной
Сей меч известен будет нам;
Что нас он обоих погубит: 400
Мне бороду мою отрубит,
Тебе главу; суди же сам,

my story's one to make you weep.
I too was once a warrior brave.
In all the bloody fights I fought
I never met a foe my equal.
If only I had never had
my younger brother to contend with!   370
That sly and spiteful Chernomór,
it's him I blame for all my anguish,
disgrace to our whole family!
At birth a dwarf, and with a beard,
from earliest youth he couldn't view
my giant frame but with vexation,
and so in his embittered heart
he came to look on me with hate.
I'd always been a bit naive,
despite my stature; while that wretch,   380
despite his idiotic build,
was devilish clever – vicious too.
What's more, mark this: to my misfortune,
in that extraordinary beard
there lurks a force of awesome magic;
so – while his beard's intact – he can
look down upon the world, betray it,
and fear no harm from anyone.
So one day he, pretending friendship,
said to me slyly: 'Listen now,   390
please do this for me – it's important.
From books about black arts I've learned
that, way beyond the eastern mountains,
upon a silent seashore, stands
a strongroom, locked and windowless,
that holds a sword, and – this is frightening –
in my dark crystal I've discerned
that an antagonistic power
intends this very sword for us,
to be the ruin of us two –   400
severing both this beard of mine
and your head. Judge, then, for yourself

Сколь важно нам приобретенье
Сего созданья злых духов!"
"Ну, что же? где тут затрудненье? –
Сказал я карле, – я готов;
Иду, хоть за пределы света".
И сосну на плечо взвалил,
А на другое для совета
Злодея брата посадил;   410
Пустился в дальнюю дорогу,
Шагал, шагал и, слава богу,
Как бы пророчеству назло,
Всё счастливо сначала шло.
За отдаленными горами
Нашли мы роковой подвал;
Я разметал его руками
И потаенный меч достал.
Но нет! судьба того хотела:
Меж нами ссора закипела –   420
И было, признаюсь, о чем!
Вопрос: кому владеть мечом?
Я спорил, карла горячился;
Бранились долго; наконец
Уловку выдумал хитрец,
Притих и будто бы смягчился.
"Оставим бесполезный спор, –
Сказал мне важно Черномор, –
Мы тем союз наш обесславим;
Рассудок в мире жить велит;   430
Судьбе решить мы предоставим,
Кому сей меч принадлежит.
К земле приникнем ухом оба
(Чего не выдумает злоба!),
И кто услышит первый звон,
Тот и владей мечом до гроба".
Сказал и лег на землю он.
Я сдуру также растянулся;
Лежу, не слышу ничего,
Смекая: обману его!   440

how vital for us both it is
to commandeer this fiendish weapon!'
'Well, what about it? Where's the problem?'
I told the dwarf. 'I'm ready; I'll go
to this earth's bounds – and even further.'
I took a pine tree on one shoulder,*
and on the other, for a guide,
I sat the dwarf, my evil brother.   410
We set out on the distant journey;
I walked and walked, and, God be thanked,
as if to spite the prophecy,
it all went famously at first.
Beyond the far-off eastern mountains
we came upon the fateful strongroom;
I tore it open with my hands
and found inside the hidden sword.
But that was that: our fate took over:
an argument boiled up between us.   420
The subject? – Well, perhaps you've guessed:
it was to whom the sword belonged.
I put my view; the dwarf grew angry;
for long we wrangled; then at length
the crafty rogue devised a trick:
he calmed down as if pacified.
'Let's put aside this pointless quarrel,'
said Chernomór in earnest tone;
'or else we'll harm the bond between us;
reason dictates we live in peace.   430
We'll leave to Fortune to decide
which one of us should own the sword.
Let's each put one ear to the ground' –
what won't an evil nature think of! –
'He that's the first to hear a sound,
that's who will own the sword for life!'
He spoke, and lay down on the ground.
Fool that I was, I stretched out too!
I lay there, couldn't hear a thing,
and thought: I'll play a trick on him!   440

Но сам жестоко обманулся.
Злодей в глубокой тишине,
Пристав, на цыпочках ко мне
Подкрался сзади, размахнулся;
Как вихорь свистнул острый меч,
И прежде, чем я оглянулся,
Уж голова слетела с плеч –
И сверхъестественная сила
В ней жизни дух остановила.
Мой остов тернием оброс;   450
Вдали, в стране, людьми забвенной,
Истлел мой прах непогребенный;
Но злобный карла перенес
Меня в сей край уединенный,
Где вечно должен был стеречь
Тобой сегодня взятый меч.
О витязь! Ты храним судьбою,*
Возьми его, и бог с тобою!
Быть может, на своем пути
Ты карлу-чародея встретишь –   460
Ах, если ты его заметишь,
Коварству, злобе отомсти!
И наконец я счастлив буду,
Спокойно мир оставлю сей –
И в благодарности моей
Твою пощечину забуду.”

But I was tricked – and cruelly!
Without the slightest noise the villain
arose, crept up on me behind
on tiptoe, lifting up his arm:
the sharp blade whistled like a whirlwind;
before I could so much as turn,
my head was sliced from off my shoulders –
but some transcendent force ordained that
this head should keep the breath of life.
In a far land unknown to man, then,   450
my trunk lies decomposed, unburied,
the bones now overgrown with thorns.
But me the evil dwarf transported
into this godforsaken place,
where everlastingly I've had
to guard the sword you've seized today.
You're under Destiny's protection,
warrior: now take it, God be with you!
Maybe, as you go on your way,
you'll come across that wizard-dwarf –   460
oh, if you do catch sight of him,
avenge his trickery and malice!
Then at the end I'll be content,
I shall depart this world in peace –
and I'll forgive with thankful grace
that punch you gave me in the face."

ПЕСНЬ ЧЕТВЕРТАЯ

Я каждый день, восстав от сна,
Благодарю сердечно Бога
За то, что в наши времена
Волшебников не так уж много.
К тому же – честь и слава им! –
Женитьбы наши безопасны...
Их замыслы не так ужасны
Мужьям, девицам молодым.*
Но есть волшебники другие,
Которых ненавижу я: 10
Улыбка, очи голубые
И голос милый – о друзья!
Не верьте им: они лукавы!
Страшитесь, подражая мне
Их упоительной отравы
И почивайте в тишине.

Поэзии чудесный гений,
Певец таинственных видений,
Любви, мечтаний и чертей,
Могил и рая верный житель,   20
И музы ветреной моей
Наперсник, пестун и хранитель!
Прости мне, северный Орфей,
Что в повести моей забавной
Теперь вослед тебе лечу
И лиру музы своенравной
Во лжи прелестной обличу.

Друзья мои, вы все слыхали,
Как бесу в древни дни злодей
Предал сперва себя с печали,   30

92

Fourth Canto

Each day, when I get up from bed,
with all my heart I thank the Lord
that in these times of ours there aren't
as many wizards as there were;
what's more – all credit to those left! –
we can be wed in safety now...
their magic gives less cause for dread
to bridegrooms and young brides alike.
There's wizardry of other sorts, though,
that I abominate – I mean   10
that smile, those eyes of blue, that voice
so amiable – but, ooh, my friends!
don't trust them; no, they'll be your ruin!
Take after me: be on your watch
for their intoxicating poison;
lie low and lead a quiet life.*

Zhukóvsky,* outstanding poet-genius,
you troubadour of mystic visions,
of love, dreams, demons, you've so truly
portrayed both death and paradise.   20
My verse is lightweight; even so
you've been my mentor, friend and guardian.
You Orpheus* of the north, forgive me
that in this flippant tale of mine
I'm following you all too closely,
flaunting my cheeky inspiration
in a facetious travesty.

My friends, I know you'll all have heard
how, once upon a time, a misfit
promised the devil in despair   30

А там и души дочерей;
Как после щедрым подаяньем,
Молитвой, верой, и постом,
И непритворным покаяньем
Снискал заступника в святом;
Как умер он и как заснули
Его двенадцать дочерей:
И нас пленили, ужаснули
Картины тайных сих ночей,
Сии чудесные виденья,   40
Сей мрачный бес, сей божий гнев,
Живые грешника мученья
И прелесть непорочных дев.
Мы с ними плакали, бродили
Вокруг зубчатых замка стен,
И сердцем тронутым любили
Их тихий сон, их тихий плен;
Душой Вадима призывали,
И пробужденье зрели их,
И часто инокинь святых   50
На гроб отцовский провожали.
И что ж, возможно ль?… нам солгали!
Но правду возвещу ли я?…*

Младой Ратмир, направя к югу
Нетерпеливый бег коня,
Уж думал пред закатом дня
Нагнать Русланову супругу.
Но день багряный вечерел;
Напрасно витязь пред собою
В туманы дальние смотрел: 60
Всё было пусто над рекою.
Зари последний луч горел
Над ярко позлащенным бором.
Наш витязь мимо черных скал
Тихонько проезжал и взором
Ночлега меж дерев искал.
Он на долину выезжает

first his, then his twelve daughters' souls;
how later through philanthropy,
through prayer, through faith in God, through fasting,
through unpretended penitence
he found a saint to intercede;
and how the old man died, and how
the twelve young daughters fell asleep:
we've felt the thrill and horror of
those eerie scenes at dead of night,
those strange and awe-inspiring visions –   40
menacing demon, angry God,
tormented sinner (true to life!),
and girls, endearing, innocent.
We've wept with them, we've roamed with them
around the castle battlements,
and we've been moved by love and pity
as soft sleep softly shackled them;
we've egged Vadím on in our minds,
and watched the girls as they awoke;
and we've walked with them when, as nuns,   50
they visited their father's tomb...
But – can it be so?... we've been lied to!
What really happened I'll now tell...

    Ratmír, Lyudmíla's youngest suitor,
had spurred his restive stallion southwards,
imagining he'd overtake
the princess before close of day.
The sky had purpled, though, then darkened,
and still Ratmír was peering forward
through rising mist to no avail: 60
both river banks were quite deserted.
As day's expiring embers glowed
catching the forest pines with gold,
our knight was riding softly by
some shadowed cliffs on lookout for
a spot to camp among the trees.
Then out into a dale he came

И видит: замок на скалах
Зубчаты стены возвышает;
Чернеют башни на углах;   70
И дева по стене высокой,
Как в море лебедь одинокий,
Идет, зарей освещена;
И девы песнь едва слышна
Долины в тишине глубокой.

1

Ложится в поле мрак ночной;
   От волн поднялся ветер хладный.
Уж поздно, путник молодой!
   Укройся в терем наш отрадный.

2

Здесь ночью нега и покой,   80
   А днем и шум и пированье.
   Приди на дружное призванье,
Приди, о путник молодой!

3

У нас найдешь красавиц рой;
   Их нежны речи и лобзанье.
   Приди на тайное призванье,
Приди, о путник молодой!

4

Тебе мы с утренней зарей
   Наполним кубок на прощанье.
   Приди на мирное призванье,   90
Приди, о путник молодой!

and spied high up upon a crag
a castle's crenellated walls,
its corner turrets silhouetted;   70
and there atop a lofty rampart,
like a lone swan upon the sea,
a girl was strolling in the half-light.
Down in the silent vale her voice
could just be heard: here's what she sang:

1

The moors grow dim at eventide;
   chill air blows off the Dnieper's waters;
come, traveller-boy, it's late to ride;
   take shelter in our homely quarters.

2

By night there's rest and comfort here;   80
   by day loud feasting fills our hall.
   We'll welcome you: come at our call;
come, traveller-boy, we're waiting here.

3

You'll find a throng of beauties here,
   who'll coax and kiss you, charmers all.
   We'll tell no tales: come at our call;
come, traveller-boy, we're waiting here.

4

When day dawns and you go from here,
   we'll fill your cup to toast us all.
   We mean no harm: come at our call;   90
come, traveller-boy, we're waiting here.

5

Ложится в поле мрак ночной;
  От волн поднялся ветер хладный.
Уж поздно, путник молодой!
  Укройся в терем наш отрадный.

Она манит, она поет;
И юный хан уж под стеною;
Его встречают у ворот
Девицы красные толпою;
При шуме ласковых речей   100
Он окружен; с него не сводят
Они пленительных очей;
Две девицы коня уводят;
В чертоги входит хан младой,
За ним отшельниц милых рой;
Одна снимает шлем крылатый,
Другая кованые латы,
Та меч берет, та пыльный щит;
Одежда неги заменит
Железные доспехи брани.   110
Но прежде юношу ведут
К великолепной русской бане.
Уж волны дымные текут
В ее серебряные чаны,
И брызжут хладные фонтаны;
Разостлан роскошью ковер;
На нем усталый хан ложится;
Прозрачный пар над ним клубится;
Потупя неги полный взор,
Прелестные, полунагие,   120
В заботе нежной и немой,
Вкруг хана девы молодые
Теснятся резвою толпой.
Над рыщарем иная машет
Ветвями молодых берез,
И жар от них душистый пашет;

5

The moors grow dim at eventide;
  chill air blows off the Dnieper's waters;
come, traveller-boy, it's late to ride;
  take shelter in our homely quarters.

She sang; and as she sang she beckoned –
and soon Ratmír's beneath the walls!
A throng of lovely girls was waiting
to greet him at the castle gates;
their words of welcome filled his ears   100
as they encircled him; they couldn't
tear their bewitching eyes away.
While two led off his horse to stable,
the young khan entered the apartments,
admiring hermit-girls in tow.
One lifted off his feathered helmet;
others undid his body mail,
or took his sword and grimy shield;
soon they would bring him leisure wear
in place of battledress of steel.   110
But first the young lad they escorted
into a splendid Russian bathhouse.
There steaming water was already
cascading into silver baths;
fine spray gushed forth from cooling fountains;
luxurious rugs bestrewed the floor.
The khan, fatigued, lay down upon them,
still visible through swirling steam.
Turning fond eyes aside, the girls,
seductive in their scanty clothing,   120
crowded excitedly around,
and overwhelmed the young Ratmír
with mute and delicate attentions.
One of them waved above the khan
a bunch of young birch twigs, with which she
wafted at him warm, scented air.

Другая соком вешних роз
Усталы члены прохлаждает
И в ароматах потопляет
Темнокудрявые власы.   130
Восторгом витязь упоенный
Уже забыл Людмилы пленной
Недавно милые красы;
Томится сладостным желаньем;
Бодрящий взор его блестит,
И, полный страстным ожиданьем,
Он тает сердцем, он горит.

    Но вот выходит он из бани,
Одетый в бархатные ткани,
В кругу прелестных дев, Ратмир   140
Садится за богатый пир.
Я не Омер: в стихах высоких
Он может воспевать один
Обеды греческих дружин,
И звон и пену чаш глубоких.
Милее, по следам Парни,
Мне славить лирою небрежной
И наготу в ночной тени,
И поцелуй любови нежной!
Луною замок озарен;   150
Я вижу терем отдаленный,
Где витязь томный, воспаленный
Вкушает одинокий сон;
Его чело, его ланиты
Мгновенным пламенем горят;
Его уста полуоткрыты
Лобзанье тайное манят;
Он страстно, медленно вздыхает,
Он видит их – и в пылком сне
Покровы к сердцу прижимает.   160
Но вот в глубокой тишине
Дверь отворилась, пол ревнивый
Скрыпит под ножкой торопливой,

Another soothed his weary limbs
with attar squeezed from vernal roses
and drenched his darkly-curling hair
in aromatic essences.   130
Ratmír, drugged with exquisite pleasure,
had put from mind the captive princess
that he'd so recently adored.
Light-headed with intense desire,
he gazed around with eyes aflame,
and, thrilling with expectant love,
he thawed within, began to burn.

    At length Ratmír emerged from bathing.
Clad in a dressing robe of velvet
and circled by entrancing girls,   140
he sat down to a sumptuous meal.
I am no Homer* – only he
could celebrate in verse sublime
the feasting of Greek warrior-lords and
the ring of their tall foaming wine cups.
My preference is, with Parny,*
to sing less solemnly the praise
of bare limbs dimly glimpsed at night,
of a soft kiss, of love itself!
The moon shone down upon the castle.   150
Yes, I can see the private guestroom
where the young warrior, flushed, exhausted,
is now in bed asleep alone;
then all at once his cheeks, his forehead
glow with a momentary flame;
at the same time his lips, half-open,
mouth an unconscious, unseen kiss;
he sighs a long and fervent sigh:
he's dreaming of the girls, and clutches
the bedclothes to his chest with passion.   160
But look! – in silence still unbroken
a door has opened; now the floor
creaks tetchily – a nimble footstep! –

И при серебряной луне
Мелькнула дева. Сны крылаты,
Сокройтесь, отлетите прочь!
Проснись – твоя настала ночь!
Проснися – дорог миг утраты!…
Она подходит, он лежит
И в сладострастной неге дремлет;   170
Покров его с одра скользит,
И жаркий пух чело объемлет.
В молчанье дева перед ним
Стоит недвижно, бездыханна,
Как лицемерная Диана
Пред милым пастырем своим;
И вот она, на ложе хана
Коленом опершись одним,
Вздохнув, лицо к нему склоняет
С томленьем, с трепетом живым,   180
И сон счастливца прерывает
Лобзаньем страстным и немым…

Но, други, девственная лира
Умолкла под моей рукой;
Слабеет робкий голос мой –
Оставим юного Ратмира;
Не смею песней продолжать:
Руслан нас должен занимать,
Руслан, сей витязь беспримерный,
В душе герой, любовник верный.   190
Упорным боем утомлен,
Под богатырской головою
Он сладостный вкушает сон.
Но вот уж раннею зарею
Сияет тихий небосклон;
Всё ясно; утра луч игривый
Главы косматый лоб златит.
Руслан встает, и конь ретивый
Уж витязя стрелою мчит.

and through a silvery ray of moonlight
a girl darts. Now's the time for dreams
to spread their wings and fly away!
Wake up – this is your night of nights!
Yes, wake up – don't waste precious moments!
The girl approached; the lad still lay there
dreaming enraptured dreams of love.   170
The covers slid from off the bed;
damp forelocks fringed his flaming temples.
The girl stood over him in silence,
she didn't move, she held her breath –
like hypocritical Diana*
standing above her shepherd-love.
The girl now moved, and on the bed
where the khan lay she leant one knee;
she breathed a sigh, then bent her head
down to him, trembling and unsteady,   180
and with a mute and hungry kiss
she cut his dream short – lucky man!

   But, friends, this harp of mine's too chaste,
it's stopped responding to my fingers;
my bashful voice is faltering too –
we'd better leave our young Ratmír;
I mustn't make these cantos too long…
Ruslán must occupy us now –
no ordinary knight, Ruslán:
by nature valiant, loyal in love.   190
Exhausted by his dogged struggle,
he now took a refreshing sleep
beside the giant warrior's head.
As soon, though, as the light of dawn
first glowed above the calm horizon,
and through the limpid air a sunbeam
touched the Head's feathered brow with gold,
Ruslán arose; and soon his steed was
speeding him arrow-like away.

И дни бегут, желтеют нивы; 200
С дерев спадает дряхлый лист;
В лесах осенний ветра свист
Певиц пернатых заглушает;
Тяжелый, пасмурный туман
Нагие холмы обвивает;
Зима приближилась – Руслан
Свой путь отважно продолжает
На дальный север; с каждым днем
Преграды новые встречает:
То бьется он с богатырем, 210
То с ведьмою, то с великаном,
То лунной ночью видит он,
Как будто сквозь волшебный сон,
Окружены седым туманом,
Русалки, тихо на ветвях
Качаясь, витязя младого
С улыбкой хитрой на устах
Манят, не говоря ни слова…
Но, тайным промыслом храним,
Бесстрашный витязь невредим; 220
В его душе желанье дремлет,
Он их не видит, им не внемлет,
Одна Людмила всюду с ним.

Но между тем, никем не зрима,
От нападений колдуна
Волшебной шапкою хранима,
Что делает моя княжна,
Моя прекрасная Людмила?
Она, безмолвна и уныла,
Одна гуляет по садам, 230
О друге мыслит и вздыхает,
Иль волю дав своим мечтам,
К родимым киевским полям
В забвенье сердца улетает;
Отца и братьев обнимает,
Подружек видит молодых

The days flew by; the fields were yellow;   200
the trees were shedding shrivelled leaves;
the song of woodland birds was smothered
beneath the whine of autumn winds;
the wooded hills, bereft of green,
were wreathed in dense and dreary fogs;
winter was near at hand. Ruslán was
pressing on bravely with his journey
to the far north, with every new day
confronting new adversities.
Once he did battle with a warrior;   210
then with a witch, an ogre next;
sometimes on moonlit nights he'd see,
as though in some enchanted dream,
rusalkas,* wreathed in hoary vapours,
who soundlessly among the boughs
swayed to and fro and smiled their knowing
smiles at young Ruslán and beckoned
him on, without explaining why...
A secret Providence, however,
preserved the fearless knight from harm   220
and lulled his appetite for love;
he looked away, he took no notice;
Lyudmíla, none else, filled his mind.

And what, meanwhile, was my Lyudmíla,
my lovely princess, up to there –
protected by that magic nightcap
from the vile wizard's molestations,
invisible to everyone?
Poor girl, companionless, dejected,
she kept meandering round the park,   230
calling Ruslán to mind and sighing.
Or, giving free rein to her dreams,
she'd fly back in oblivion
to her dear Kiev countryside,
to give a hug to father, brothers,
to meet once more her childhood playmates,

И старых мамушек своих –
Забыты плен и разлученье!
Но вскоре бедная княжна
Свое теряет заблужденье   240
И вновь уныла и одна.
Рабы влюбленного злодея,
И день и ночь, сидеть не смея,
Меж тем по замку, по садам
Прелестной пленницы искали,
Метались, громко призывали,
Однако все по пустякам.
Людмила ими забавлялась:
В волшебных рощах иногда
Без шапки вдруг она являлась   250
И кликала: "Сюда, сюда!"
И все бросались к ней толпою;
Но в сторону – незрима вдруг –
Она неслышною стопою
От хищных убегала рук.
Везде всечасно замечали
Ее минутные следы:
То позлащенные плоды
На шумных ветвях исчезали,
То капли ключевой воды   260
На луг измятый упадали:
Тогда наверно в замке знали,
Что пьет иль кушает княжна.
На ветвях кедра иль березы
Скрываясь по ночам, она
Минутного искала сна –
Но только проливала слезы,
Звала супруга и покой,
Томилась грустью и зевотой,
И редко, редко пред зарей,   270
Склонясь ко древу головой,
Дремала тонкою дремотой;
Едва редела ночи мгла,
Людмила к водопаду шла

and greet old nannies whom she'd loved,
forgetting distance and duress.
Soon, though, the sad princess came back
to earth, recalling where she was now,   240
again dejected and alone.
Meanwhile the love-crazed wizard's slaves
dared not take rest, but night and day
kept searching park and castle for
the precious prisoner who'd vanished;
they dashed around, they called out loud,
but all their efforts came to nothing.
Lyudmíla had some fun with them:
sometimes within the enchanted woods,
capless, she'd let herself be noticed;   250
she'd cry aloud: "This way, yes, this way!";
and they'd all rush at her together;
then, suddenly unseen again
and unheard, she'd begin to run,
dodge sideways, and evade their clutches.
Now here, now there, they'd keep observing
some momentary sign of her:
maybe some golden oranges
would disappear from creaking boughs;
or else pure drops of fountain water   260
would splash onto the crumpled grass:
the castle folk would know from this
that she'd been taking food or drink.
At nights she tried to snatch a nap
upon a hidden bed of twigs
beneath a cedar tree or birch –
but tears were all that came to her;
weary of loneliness and yawning,
she'd cry for husband, cry for sleep;
then fitfully before the dawn   270
she'd lean her head against the tree
and lapse into a shallow doze.
As soon as night began to fade,
she'd go off to a waterfall

Умыться хладною струею:
Сам карла утренней порою
Однажды видел из палат,
Как под невидимой рукою
Плескал и брызгал водопад.
С своей обычною тоскою   280
До новой ночи, здесь и там,
Она бродила по садам:
Нередко под вечер слыхали
Ее приятный голосок;
Нередко в рощах поднимали
Иль ею брошенный венок,
Или клочки персидской шали,
Или заплаканный платок.

Жестокой страстью уязвленный,
Досадой, злобой омраченный,   290
Колдун решился наконец
Поймать Людмилу непременно.
Так Лемноса хромой кузнец,
Прияв супружеский венец
Из рук прелестной Цитереи,
Раскинул сеть ее красам,
Открыв насмешливым богам
Киприды нежные затеи…

Скучая, бедная княжна
В прохладе мраморной беседки   300
Сидела тихо близ окна
И сквозь колеблемые ветки
Смотрела на цветущий луг.
Вдруг слышит – кличут: "Милый друг!"
И видит верного Руслана.
Его черты, походка, стан;
Но бледен он, в очах туман,
И на бедре живая рана –
В ней сердце дрогнуло. "Руслан!
Руслан!… он точно!" И стрелою   310

to wash herself in icy water:
one of those mornings Chernomór
himself out of a palace window
saw the cascade of water breaking
and splashing on an unseen hand.
From then until the next night came   280
she'd wander, sick at heart as ever,
this way and that around the grounds.
At times towards the end of day
they'd hear her pleasant voice half-singing;
at times too in the woods they'd find
a daisy chain she'd tossed aside,
some wool plucked from a Persian stole,
or a silk hanky steeped in tears.

    Gnawed by his unrelenting lust,
humiliated, riled and sullen,   290
the wizard finally resolved
to catch Lyudmíla, come what may.
Just so did the lame blacksmith-god,
who'd taken for his goddess-wife
the too-attractive Aphrodite,
spread nets to entrap her errant charms,
and so exposed her escapades
to all the gods – and how they laughed!*

    Bored now, the poor princess was sitting
for shade within a summerhouse   300
of marble, by an aperture,
and through the swaying tree boughs she
looked out onto a flowered field.
A voice! "Dear friend", someone was calling.
She saw Ruslán – yes, surely him!
The face was his, the walk, the stature;
but he was pale and misty-eyed,
and in his thigh an open wound!
Her heart was pounding – "Oh, Ruslán!
Ruslán! It's him!" And like an arrow   310

109

К супругу пленница летит,
В слезах, трепеща, говорит:
"Ты здесь… ты ранен… что с тобою?"
Уже достигла, обняла:
О ужас… призрак исчезает!
Княжна в сетях; с ее чела
На землю шапка упадает.
Хладея, слышит грозный крик:
"Она моя!" – и в тот же миг
Зрит колдуна перед очами.   320
Раздался девы жалкий стон,
Падет без чувств – и дивный сон
Объял несчастную крылами.

    Что будет с бедною княжной?
О страшный вид: волшебник хилый
Ласкает дерзостной рукой
Младые прелести Людмилы!
Ужели счастлив будет он?
Чу… вдруг раздался рога звон,*
И кто-то карлу вызывает.   330
В смятенье, бледный чародей
На деву шапку надевает;
Трубят опять; звучней, звучней!
И он летит к безвестной встрече,
Закинув бороду за плечи.

the prisoner flew to join her husband,
saying, in tears, with broken voice:
"You're here... you're injured... How? What's happened?"
She reached him, threw her arms around him:
then – aah! – he disappeared – a phantom!
Nets closed around her. From her head
the nightcap tumbled to the ground.
She froze with terror, heard a shriek,
"Here she is – mine!", and then and there
in front of her saw Chernomór.   320
She uttered a pathetic cry,
fell senseless – then a magic sleep
enwrapped the poor girl in its wings.

   What next for the unlucky princess?
Oh dreadful sight – the feeble wizard
caressing with his shameless hands
Lyudmíla's young and lovely figure!
Surely the wizard won't win through?
Hark, though!... A sudden horn call sounded –
someone was challenging the dwarf!   330
Perplexed and pallid, Chernomór
put the cap back upon Lyudmíla.
More horn calls, louder – louder still!
And to an unsure rendezvous,
beard tossed behind him, off he flew.

ПЕСНЬ ПЯТАЯ

Ах, как мила моя княжна!
Мне нрав ее всего дороже:
Она чувствительна, скромна,
Любви супружеской верна,
Немножко ветрена… так что же?
Еще милее тем она.
Всечасно прелестию новой
Умеет нас она пленить;
Скажите: можно ли сравнить
Ее с Дельфирою суровой?   10
Одной – судьба послала дар
Обворожать сердца и взоры;
Ее улыбка, разговоры
Во мне любви рождают жар.
А та – под юбкою гусар,
Лишь дайте ей усы да шпоры!
Блажен, кого под вечерок
В уединенный уголок
Моя Людмила поджидает
И другом сердца назовет;   20
Но, верьте мне, блажен и тот,
Кто от Дельфиры убегает
И даже с нею незнаком.

Да, впрочем, дело не о том!
Но кто трубил? Кто чародея
На сечу грозну вызывал?
Кто колдуна перепугал?
Руслан. Он, местью пламенея,
Достиг обители злодея.
Уж витязь под горой стоит,   30
Призывный рог, как буря, воет,

Fifth Canto

How fond I am of my princess!
Her nature I can't prize too highly:
she's sensitive and unassuming,
loyal and loving as a wife,
a little scatterbrained… but so what? –
all the more likeable for that.
She has a way of constantly
finding new charms with which to enthral us.
Now, tell me: how can you compare her
with that formidable Delphíra?*   10
Lyudmíla has a heaven-sent gift for
bewitching every heart and eye;
her unforced smile, her chitter-chatter,
ignite in me a glow of love.
The other is, beneath her skirt,
a horse guard – less moustache and spurs!
Lucky's the man who finds Lyudmíla
waiting for him as evening falls
in a secluded spot, and hears
her calling him "my dearest friend";   20
but that chap's lucky too, trust me,
who has escaped Delphíra's clutches
or, better still, has never met her!

   But – sorry! – that's beside the point.
Who'd blown the horn, then? Who was calling
the wizard out to mortal combat?
Who'd frightened him beyond his wits?
Ruslán it was! Ablaze for vengeance,
he'd found the villain's hideaway.
Halting below the castle rock, he'd   30
blasted a challenge on his horn;

Нетерпеливый конь кипит
И снег копытом мочным роет.
Князь карлу ждет. Внезапно он
По шлему крепкому стальному
Рукой незримой поражен;
Удар упал подобно грому;
Руслан подъемлет смутный взор
И видит – прямо над главою –
С подъятой, страшной булавою   40
Летает карла Черномор.
Щитом покрывшись, он нагнулся,
Мечом потряс и замахнулся;
Но тот взвился под облака;
На миг исчез – и свысока
Шумя летит на князя снова.
Проворный витязь отлетел,
И в снег с размаха рокового
Колдун упал – да там и сел;
Руслан, не говоря ни слова,   50
С коня долой, к нему спешит,
Поймал, за бороду хватает,
Волшебник силится, кряхтит
И вдруг с Русланом улетает…
Ретивый конь вослед глядит;
Уже колдун под облаками;
На бороде герой висит;
Летят над мрачными лесами,
Летят над дикими горами,
Летят над бездною морской;   60
От напряженья костенея,
Руслан за бороду злодея
Упорной держится рукой.
Меж тем, на воздухе слабея
И силе русской изумясь,
Волшебник гордому Руслану
Коварно молвит: "Слушай, князь!
Тебе вредить я перестану;
Младое мужество любя,

his horse meanwhile tossed fretfully,
stabbing the snow with sturdy hoofs.
He waited – then an arm unseen
struck him an unexpected blow
on his strong helmet forged of steel,
smiting it like a thunderbolt.
Dazed as he was, Ruslán looked upward
and saw, directly overhead,
flying with fearsome bludgeon brandished,   40
the evil wizard-dwarf himself.
He ducked and raised his shield for cover,
grasped his sword tight and thrust it high.
The wizard whirled up to the clouds,
vanished a moment, then once more
swooped with a whoosh upon the prince.
Ruslán dodged deftly to the side.
At death-defying speed the dwarf
crashed in the snow, and sat there stunned;
Ruslán said not a word, but quickly   50
dismounted, dashed at his assailant,
caught him and clasped him by the beard.
The dwarf whined, wrestled, then without a
warning flew off, Ruslán in tow...
The horse looked on in agitation;
soon Chernomór had reached the clouds,
Ruslán still dangling from the beard.
They flew above dark-shadowed forests,
they flew above wild mountain wastes,
they flew above unfathomed oceans.   60
Though stiff and numb from the exertion
Ruslán maintained his stubborn grip
on the malign magician's whiskers.
Meanwhile, the wizard, weakened by
the strain of flying, and astonished
at a Russian's strength and at Ruslán's
audacity, said slyly: "Prince,
listen, I'll cease to feud with you;
I relish manliness and youth:

Забуду всё, прощу тебя,   70
Спущусь – но только с уговором…"
"Молчи, коварный чародей! –
Прервал наш витязь, – с Черномором,
С мучителем жены своей,
Руслан не знает договора!
Сей грозный меч накажет вора.
Лети хоть до ночной звезды,
А быть тебе без бороды!"
Боязнь объемлет Черномора;
В досаде, в горести немой,   80
Напрасно длинной бородой
Усталый карла потрясает:
Руслан ее не выпускает
И щиплет волосы порой.

Два дни колдун героя носит,
На третий он пощады просит:
"О, рыцарь, сжалься надо мной;
Едва дышу; нет мочи боле;
Оставь мне жизнь, в твоей я воле;
Скажи – спущусь, куда велишь…"   90
"Теперь ты наш: ага, дрожишь!
Смирись, покорствуй русской силе!
Неси меня к моей Людмиле".
Смиренно внемлет Черномор;
Домой он с витязем пустился;
Летит – и мигом очутился
Среди своих ужасных гор.

Тогда Руслан одной рукою
Взял меч сраженной головы
И, бороду схватив другою,   100
Отсек ее, как горсть травы.
"Знай наших! – молвил он жестоко, –
Что, хищник, где твоя краса?
Где сила?" – и на шлем высокий
Седые вяжет волоса;

I'll willingly forgive, forget;   70
I'll come to earth – but only if…"
"Shut up, you crafty sorcerer,"
Ruslán cut in. "With Chernomór,
my wife's tormentor, I don't mean
to start discussing 'ifs' and 'buts'!
This dreaded sword will trounce you, thief.
Fly to the pole star, if you like –
but lose your beard you will, for sure!"
Then terror seized the wizard-dwarf.
Speechless with anger and vexation,   80
and tiring now, he tried in vain
to shake the knight from off his beard.
Ruslán would not relax his grip –
he even sometimes tweaked the hairs.

   The wizard dragged him on for two days,
but on the third he sued for peace:
"Distinguished knight, have mercy on me;
I'm out of breath; my strength has gone;
grant me my life; I'm in your power;
speak – and I'll land where you command…"   90
"Aha, you're rattled – cowed at last!
Meekly concede: the Russian's won!
So take me now to my Lyudmíla."
Then meekly Chernomór obeyed,
and set off home with Prince Ruslán;
he flew – and very soon he'd landed
back in his awesome mountain realm.

   At once Ruslán took up in one hand
the sword the vanquished Head had guarded;
grasping the whiskers with the other   100
he cropped them like a clump of grass.
He snarled: 'Don't underrate a Russian!
Girl-snatcher, where's your pride and joy now,
source of your power?" And to his tall
helmet he tied the grizzled beard.

Свистя зовет коня лихого;
Веселый конь летит и ржет;
Наш витязь карлу чуть живого
В котомку за седло кладет,
А сам, боясь мгновенья траты,   110
Спешит на верх горы крутой,
Достиг, и с радостной душой
Летит в волшебные палаты.
Вдали завидя шлем брадатый,
Залог победы роковой,
Пред ним арапов чудный рой,
Толпы невольниц боязливых,
Как призраки, со всех сторон
Бегут – и скрылись. Ходит он
Один средь храмин горделивых,   120
Супругу милую зовет –
Лишь эхо сводов молчаливых
Руслану голос подает;
В волненье чувств нетерпеливых
Он отворяет двери в сад –
Идет, идет – и не находит;
Кругом смущенный взор обводит –
Всё мертво: рощицы молчат,
Беседки пусты; на стремнинах,
Вдоль берегов ручья, в долинах,   130
Нигде Людмилы следу нет,
И ухо ничего не внемлет.
Внезапный князя хлад объемлет,
В очах его темнеет свет,
В уме возникли мрачны думы…
"Быть может, горесть… плен угрюмый…
Минута… волны…" В сих мечтах
Он погружен. С немой тоскою
Поникнул витязь головою;
Его томит невольный страх;   140
Недвижим он, как мертвый камень;
Мрачится разум; дикий пламень
И яд отчаянной любви

He whistled for his eager horse,
who ran up cheerfully and whinnied.
Ruslán then stuffed the dwarf, half-dead now,
into his saddle bag. Himself,
he rushed up the steep castle rock,   110
afraid to lose one moment more.
Once there, full of expectant joy,
he flew into the magic palace.
At his approach the slaves in throngs –
exotic negroes, timid maids –
who'd spied far off the bearded helmet
and guessed from that the knight's success,
scurried off everywhere like phantoms –
and vanished. Left alone, Ruslán
strode round the grandiose apartments,   120
calling to his beloved wife –
no answer came, though, from the hush
of those high chambers, save his echo.
Emotional, impatient, anxious,
he thrust the garden doors apart,
walked on, walked on, again found nothing.
He gazed around in consternation –
no sign of life: throughout the park
woodlands were still, gazebos empty;
on slopes, by banks of brooks, in dells –   130
nowhere a trace of his Lyudmíla,
nowhere a sound to lead him on.
He felt a sudden chill enfold him,
light turned to darkness in his eyes,
grim thoughts welled up within his mind…
"Could anguish… harsh detention… just for
one moment… in the pool?…" Ideas
like this engulfed him. Shattered, dumbstruck,
the warrior hung his head in grief.
Ungovernable dread assailed him;   140
he stood stock still, inert as stone;
his wits were dimmed; the fiercely flaming
virulence of despairing love

Уже текут в его крови.
Казалось – тень княжны прекрасной
Коснулась трепетным устам…
И вдруг, неистовый, ужасный,
Стремится витязь по садам;
Людмилу с воплем призывает,
С холмов утесы отрывает,   150
Всё рушит, всё крушит мечом –
Беседки, рощи упадают,
Древа, мосты в волнах ныряют ,
Степь обнажается кругом!
Далеко гулы повторяют
И рев, и треск, и шум, и гром;
Повсюду меч звенит и свищет,
Прелестный край опустошен –
Безумный витязь жертвы ищет,
С размаха вправо, влево он   160
Пустынный воздух рассекает…
И вдруг – нечаянный удар
С княжны невидимой сбивает
Прощальный Черномора дар…
Волшебства вмиг исчезла сила:
В сетях открылася Людмила!

Не веря сам своим очам,
Нежданным счастьем упоенный,
Наш витязь падает к ногам
Подруги верной, незабвенной,   170
Целует руки, сети рвет,
Любви, восторга слезы льет,
Зовет ее – но дева дремлет,
Сомкнуты очи и уста,
И сладострастная мечта
Младую грудь ее подъемлет.
Руслан с нее не сводит глаз,
Его терзает вновь кручина…
Но вдруг знакомый слышит глас,
Глас добродетельного Финна: 180
"Мужайся, князь! В обратный путь

came flooding swiftly through his veins.
Then seemingly Lyudmíla's shadow
caressed his quivering lips with hers...
Ruslán now ran amok, careering,
frenzied and fearsome, through the park;
in broken cries he called the princess;
great rocks he wrenched from sides of hills; 150
all he could reach he smashed, he shattered –
gazebos tumbled, thickets toppled;
trees, bridges fell, blocked pools and channels;
the encircling wastelands lay exposed;
and roar and rumble, blast and boom
reverberated far around.
His heedless sword kept whistling, clanging;
the lovely park lay ravaged, wrecked –
the maddened warrior craved a victim.
With all his might to right, to left, 160
he sliced and slashed the empty air.
Then suddenly a random stroke
knocked from unseen Lyudmíla's head
the wizard's parting present to her...
the spell was broken in an instant:
there was Lyudmíla swathed in nets!

Ruslán could not believe his eyes;
elated by unlooked-for joy,
he fell at the princess's feet –
his friend, still loyal, still as remembered! – 170
he kissed her hands, tore at the netting,
shed tears of love, of ecstasy;
he called her name – but she was slumbering,
her eyes, her mouth remained fast shut;
she dreamt, though, of her heart's desire,
which made her young breast rise and fall.
Ruslán regarded her intently,
torn now by new anxiety...
but then he heard a voice he knew,
the voice – yes! – of the kindly Finn: 180
"Courage, Ruslán! Set off for home,

Ступай со спящею Людмилой;
Наполни сердце новой силой,
Любви и чести верен будь.
Небесный гром на злобу грянет,
И воцарится тишина –
И в светлом Киеве княжна
Перед Владимиром восстанет
От очарованного сна."
Руслан, сим гласом оживленный,   190
Берет в объятия жену,
И тихо с ношей драгоценной
Он оставляет вышину
И сходит в дол уединенный.

В молчанье, с карлой за седлом,
Поехал он своим путем;
В его руках лежит Людмила,
Свежа, как вешняя заря,
И на плечо богатыря
Лицо спокойное склонила.   200
Власами, свитыми в кольцо,
Пустынный ветерок играет;
Как часто грудь ее вздыхает!
Как часто тихое лицо
Мгновенной розою пылает!
Любовь и тайная мечта
Русланов образ ей приносят,
И с томным шепотом уста
Супруга имя произносят...
В забвенье сладком ловит он   210
Ее волшебное дыханье,
Улыбку, слезы, нежный стон
И сонных персей волнованье...

Меж тем, по долам, по горам,
И в белый день, и по ночам,
Наш витязь едет непрестанно.
Еще далек предел желанный,

and take Lyudmíla with you sleeping;
renew your strength, refresh your heart;
be true to love, be true to knighthood.
Heaven's thunderbolt will fall on malice,
tranquillity will reign at last –
and once Princess Lyudmíla's back
in lustrous Kiev with her father,
she'll wake from her enchanted sleep."
This voice gave new life to Ruslán;   190
he took his wife up in his arms,
and gently, with his precious load,
he left the lofty castle for
the lonely valley far below.

    In silence, dwarf in saddle bag,
Ruslán commenced his journey homeward;
Lyudmíla rested in his arms,
fresh as a dawning day in springtime,
her head reclining peacefully
upon her valiant champion's shoulder.   200
Her hair, still gathered in a clasp,
was ruffled by the steppe-land breeze;
and often did she heave a sigh,
and often did her gentle face
burn with a momentary blush!
Her love, her private dreams, were bringing
before her mind her husband's image,
and she would somnolently murmur
through half-closed lips the name "Ruslán"...
Oblivious to all else, he marked   210
with joy each miracle of breathing,
each smile and tear, each gentle sigh,
each stirring of her slumbering breast...

    And all the while, by dale and hill,
in brilliant daylight and in darkness,
Ruslán rode on without a break.
The home he longed for lay far off still;

А дева спит. Но юный князь,
Бесплодным пламенем томясь,
Ужель, страдалец постоянный,   220
Супругу только сторожил
И в целомудренном мечтанье,
Смирив нескромное желанье,
Свое блаженство находил?
Монах, который сохранил
Потомству верное преданье
О славном витязе моем,
Нас уверяет смело в том;
И верю я! Без разделенья
Унылы, грубы наслажденья: 230
Мы прямо счастливы вдвоем.
Пастушки, сон княжны прелестной
Не походил на ваши сны,
Порой томительной весны,
На мураве, в тени древесной.
Я помню маленький лужок
Среди березовой дубравы,
Я помню темный вечерок,
Я помню Лиды сон лукавый…
Ах, первый поцелуй любви,   240
Дрожащий, легкий, торопливый,
Не разогнал, друзья мои,
Ее дремоты терпеливой…
Но полно, я болтаю вздор!
К чему любви воспоминанье?
Ее утеха и страданье
Забыты мною с давних пор;
Теперь влекут мое вниманье
Княжна, Руслан и Черномор.

    Пред ними стелется равнина,   250
Где ели изредка взошли;
И грозного холма вдали
Чернеет круглая вершина
Небес на яркой синеве.

the girl still slept. The youthful prince's
desire blazed on without fulfilment,
tormenting him, a martyr ever –   220
but did he really just keep watch
over his wife, and find his solace
in thoughts of love, without the deed,
subduing all his grosser instincts?
The monk* who faithfully preserved
the record of our famous knight
and left it for posterity
assures us firmly that is so:
and I believe him! Unshared pleasures,
you know, are shabby, shoddy pleasures: 230
we're truly happy two together.
Lyudmíla's sleep was different from
the sleep those shepherdesses sleep
under the trees, upon the grass,
in springtime's enervating season.
I call to mind a pretty glade
amid a wood of silver birch;
I call to mind a pretty sunset,
dusk falling, Lída* feigning sleep…
ah, when I gave her my first kiss –   240
a timid, fleeting, hurried kiss –
she didn't let it waken her,
my friends, from her expectant slumbers…
But that's enough: I'm blabbing nonsense!
What good is it remembering love?
The fun love gave me, and the pain –
both long ago I put from mind;
what's now demanding my attention
is prince, princess, and Chernomór.

   Before them now there stretched a plain,   250
from which some scattered fir trees rose;
and in the distance there appeared,
quite black against the bright blue sky,
a beetling hillock's rounded crown.

Руслан глядит – и догадался,
Что подъезжает к голове;
Быстрее борзый конь помчался;
Уж видно чудо из чудес;
Она глядит недвижным оком;
Власы ее как черный лес,   260
Поросший на челе высоком;
Ланиты жизни лишены,
Свинцовой бледностью покрыты,
Уста огромные открыты,
Огромны зубы стеснены…
Над полумертвой головою
Последний день уж тяготел.
К ней храбрый витязь прилетел
С Людмилой, с карлой за спиною.
Он крикнул: "Здравствуй, голова!   270
Я здесь! наказан твой изменник!
Гляди: вот он, злодей наш пленник!"
И князя гордые слова
Ее внезапно оживили.
На миг в ней чувство разбудили,
Очнулась будто ото сна,
Взглянула, страшно застонала…
Узнала витязя она
И брата с ужасом узнала.
Надулись ноздри; на щеках   280
Багровый огнь еще родился,
И в умирающих глазах
Последний гнев изобразился.
В смятенье, в бешенстве немом
Она зубами скрежетала
И брату хладным языком
Укор невнятный лепетала…*
Уже ее в тот самый час
Кончалось долгое страданье:
Чела мгновенный пламень гас,   290
Слабело тяжкое дыханье,
Огромный закатился взор,

As Ruslán looked, he realized
that he was drawing near the Head;
the nimble steed sped even faster;
and soon they saw the prodigy.
The Head was staring, eyes unblinking,
high forehead overhung with hair   260
as if a dense, dark forest grew there;
the cheeks were drained of life and showed
a greyish pallor as of lead;
the massive mouth was gaping open;
the massive teeth were tightly clenched...
over the Head, half-dead already,
life's last grim day was looming now.
The brave knight galloped up, still bearing
Lyudmíla, with the dwarf behind.
He shouted: "Greetings, Head! I'm back!   270
The one who cheated you's been punished!
Look: here he is; we've caught the wretch!"
These words of triumph from the prince
revivified the Head at once
and for a moment stirred its senses.
It roused itself as if from sleep,
looked up – and gave a fearsome snort...
the Head had recognized Ruslán,
had recognized its brother too,
with outrage – for its nostrils flared,   280
its cheeks regained a purplish glow,
and in its eyes so near to death
there flickered one last flash of fury.
Distraught, and stricken dumb with rage,
the Head began to grind its teeth,
and with a tongue now cold it mouthed
a muffled curse against its brother...
In that same hour the Head's protracted
torment was drawing to an end:
the face's momentary flush   290
died down; the heavy breathing slackened;
the light of the huge eyes went out;

И вскоре князь и Черномор
Узрели смерти содроганье...
Она почила вечным сном.
В молчанье витязь удалился;
Дрожащий карлик за седлом
Не смел дышать, не шевелился
И чернокнижным языком
Усердно демонам молился.   300

На склоне темных берегов
Какой-то речки безымянной,
В прохладном сумраке лесов,
Стоял поникшей хаты кров,
Густыми соснами венчанный.
В теченье медленном река
Вблизи плетень из тростника
Волною сонной омывала
И вкруг него едва журчала
При легком шуме ветерка.   310
Долина в сих местах таилась,
Уединенна и темна;
И там, казалось, тишина
С начала мира воцарилась.
Руслан остановил коня.
Всё было тихо, безмятежно;
От рассветающего дня
Долина с рощею прибрежной
Сквозь утренний сияла дым.
Руслан на луг жену слагает,   320
Садится близ нее, вздыхает
С уныньем сладким и немым;
И вдруг он видит пред собою
Смиренный парус челнока
И слышит песню рыбака
Над тихоструйною рекою.
Раскинув невод по волнам,
Рыбак, на весла наклоненный,
Плывет к лесистым берегам,

and soon the prince and Chernomór
witnessed the shudder that spelled death.
The Head was now at rest for ever.
In silence Prince Ruslán rode off.
Behind the saddle, terrified,
the dwarf dared neither move nor breathe
and in an occult language uttered
a fervent prayer to evil powers.   300

    A deeply shadowed bank sloped down
to a small river yet unnamed;
there in the forest's cooling half-light
beneath a canopy of pines
stood a dilapidated cottage.
The river flowed by sluggishly
and lapped with soporific plashes
against a screen of plaited rush –
though you could scarcely hear the splashing
over the rustle of the breeze.   310
The valley hereabouts was lonely,
secluded, and engulfed in shade;
stillness had seemingly held sway there
since the inception of the world.
Ruslán had reined his stallion in.
The place was peaceful, undisturbed;
vale, river, overhanging woods
reflected through an early haze
the radiance of the dawning day.
He laid his wife upon the grass   320
and, sitting by her, heaved a sigh
of sorrow and of wordless love.
Then he caught sight, to his surprise,
of a small boat with makeshift sail
and heard across the placid stream
the singing of a fisherman.
The fisherman had moored his nets
in the mid-river and was now
rowing towards the wooded bank,

К порогу хижины смиренной.   330
И видит добрый князь Руслан:
Челнок ко брегу приплывает;
Из темной хаты выбегает
Младая дева; стройный стан,
Власы, небрежно распущенны,
Улыбка, тихий взор очей,
И грудь, и плечи обнаженны,
Всё мило, всё пленяет в ней.
И вот они, обняв друг друга,
Садятся у прохладных вод,   340
И час беспечного досуга
Для них с любовью настает.
Но в изумленье молчаливом
Кого же в рыбаке счастливом
Наш юный витязь узнает?
Хазарский хан, избранный славой,
Ратмир, в любви, в войне кровавой
Его соперник молодой,
Ратмир в пустыне безмятежной
Людмилу, славу позабыл   350
И им навеки изменил
В объятиях подруги нежной.

Герой приближился, и вмиг
Отшельник узнает Руслана,
Встает, летит. Раздался крик…
И обнял князь младого хана.
"Что вижу я? – спросил герой, –
Зачем ты здесь, зачем оставил
Тревоги жизни боевой
И меч, который ты прославил?"   360
"Мой друг, – ответствовал рыбак, –
Душе наскучил бранной славы
Пустой и гибельный призрак.
Поверь: невинные забавы,
Любовь и мирные дубравы
Милее сердцу во сто крат.

bound for the humble cottage there. 330
As the prince watched with kindly interest,
the little vessel reached the shore;
and from the cottage out there ran
a pretty lass: her graceful figure,
her hair, left simple and unbraided,
her smiling lips, her gentle eyes,
bosom, bare shoulders – every feature
of hers was charming, captivating.
As he looked on, the pair embraced
and sat by the refreshing waters: 340
now was their time for relaxation,
for recreation, and for love.
Ruslán was silently amazed
in the blithe fisherman he saw
to recognize none other than
the far-famed Khazar khan Ratmír,
the one who'd been his youthful rival
in bloody combat and in love.
In this calm backwater Ratmír
had put aside fame and Lyudmíla, 350
renouncing both for evermore,
to rest in his fond girlfriend's arms.

The prince approached them. The recluse
identified Ruslán at once;
he rose, ran to him. Cries of pleasure!
Ruslán embraced the young Ratmír:
"What's this I see?" the warrior asked,
"Why are you here? Why've you abandoned
your soldier's life of high adventure
and your celebrity as swordsman?" 360
"My friend," the fisherman replied,
"I've tired of military ambition –
a mirage meaningless, malign.
Trust me: innocuous amusements,
human affection, peaceful woods are
a hundred times more satisfying.

Теперь, утратив жажду брани,
Престал платить безумству дани,
И, верным счастием богат,
Я всё забыл, товарищ милый,   370
Всё, даже прелести Людмилы.”
“Любезный хан, я очень рад! –
Сказал Руслан, – она со мною”.
“Возможно ли, какой судьбою?
Что слышу? Русская княжна…
Она с тобою, где ж она?
Позволь… но нет, боюсь измены;
Моя подруга мне мила;
Моей счастливой перемены
Она виновницей была;   380
Она мне жизнь, она мне радость!
Она мне возвратила вновь
Мою утраченную младость,
И мир, и чистую любовь.
Напрасно счастье мне сулили
Уста волшебниц молодых;
Двенадцать дев меня любили:
Я для нее покинул их;
Оставил терем их веселый,
В тени хранительных дубров;   390
Сложил и меч и шлем тяжелый,
Забыл и славу и врагов.
Отшельник, мирный и безвестный,
Остался в счастливой глуши,
С тобой, друг милый, друг прелестный,
С тобою, свет моей души!”
Пастушка милая внимала
Друзей открытый разговор,
И, устремив на хана взор,
И улыбалась, и вздыхала.   400

   Рыбак и витязь на брегах
До темной ночи просидели
С душой и сердцем на устах –

Now that I've lost my thirst for conflict,
I've ceased to pay a fee to madness;
instead, I'm rich with real joy now;
I've put the past behind me – even,   370
dear friend, my fondness for Lyudmíla."
"Good for you, Khan – I'm glad of that!"
exclaimed Ruslán. "She's here with me."
"No, surely not – how could she be?
Did I mishear?... The Russian princess?...
She's here with you? Where is she then?
Let me... But no, I'd better not.
I'm too fond of my girlfriend here;
she is the one who's brought about
the happy change you see in me;   380
she's now my life, she's now my joy!
It's she who's now restored to me
my youth – the youth that I had wasted –
my peace of mind, my selfless love.
The bliss that those young charmers' kisses
had promised was no bliss at all.
There were twelve girls in love with me:
but I forsook them for this one;
their festive palace, sheltered by
protective oak woods, I abandoned;   390
I doffed my sword, my massive helmet,
forgot ambition and my foes.
And here I am, contented now,
a peaceable, obscure recluse,
in this remote spot here with you, dear,
with you, sweet friend, my life's bright star!"
The pretty country lass had listened
to the two friends' frank conversation,
her eyes fixed ever on the khan,
with now a smile, and now a sigh.   400

 They sat on, fisherman and knight,
upon the bank till darkness fell,
speaking of matters deep and heartfelt,

Часы невидимо летели.
Чернеет лес, темна гора;
Встает луна – всё тихо стало;
Герою в путь давно пора.
Накинув тихо покрывало
На деву спящую, Руслан
Идет и на коня садится;   410
Задумчиво безмолвный хан
Душой вослед ему стремится,
Руслану счастия, побед,
И славы, и любви желает…
И думы гордых, юных лет
Невольной грустью оживляет…

Зачем судьбой не суждено
Моей непостоянной лире
Геройство воспевать одно
И с ним (незнаемые в мире)   420
Любовь и дружбу старых лет?
Печальной истины поэт,
Зачем я должен для потомства
Порок и злобу обнажать
И тайны козни вероломства
В правдивых песнях обличать?

Княжны искатель недостойный,
Охоту к славе потеряв,
Никем не знаемый, Фарлаф
В пустыне дальной и спокойной   430
Скрывался и Наины ждал.
И час торжественный настал.
К нему волшебница явилась,
Вещая: "Знаешь ли меня?
Ступай за мной; седлай коня!"
И ведьма кошкой обратилась;
Оседлан конь, она пустилась;
Тропами мрачными дубрав
За нею следует Фарлаф.

as hours unnoticed sped away.
Black grew the forest, dim the hills;
the moon rose; all around was hushed;
our knight should long ago have left.
Spreading a blanket quietly
over the sleeping girl, Ruslán
moved now and sat astride his stallion.   410
The silent khan stood deep in thought and
longed in his heart of hearts to follow;
he wished Ruslán all happiness –
triumphs, and high renown, and love...
and with involuntary regret
called back to mind his young ambitions...

My subject-matter's all too varied –
oh, how I wish it were my gift
to celebrate, uniquely, valour
and with it – what's unknown today –   420
old-fashioned love and fellowship!
But, sadly, I'm a poet of
the real world, and I must tell
posterity of vice and malice,
and in my truthful verse unmask
a traitor and his machinations.

The princess's unworthy suitor,
Farláf, then, unbeknown to all,
his appetite for glory lost,
was skulking in obscurity   430
back home and waiting for Naína.
At last his hour of triumph came.
The sorceress appeared before him
and spoke: "You know who I am, don't you?
Saddle your horse and follow me."
The witch then turned into a she-cat,
and, horse once saddled, headed off
by shadowed pathways through the forest,
herself in front, Farláf behind.

Долина тихая дремала,   440
В ночной одетая туман,
Луна во мгле перебегала
Из тучи в тучу и курган
Мгновенным блеском озаряла.
Под ним в безмолвии Руслан
Сидел с обычною тоскою
Пред усыпленною княжною.
Глубоку думу думал он,
Мечты летели за мечтами,
И неприметно веял сон   450
Над ним холодными крылами.
На деву смутными очами
В дремоте томной он взглянул
И, утомленною главою
Склонясь к ногам ее, заснул.

 И снится вещий сон герою:
Он видит, будто бы княжна
Над страшной бездны глубиною
Стоит недвижна и бледна…
И вдруг Людмила исчезает,   460
Стоит один над бездной он…
Знакомый глас, призывный стон
Из тихой бездны вылетает…
Руслан стремится за женой;
Стремглав летит во тьме глубокой…
И видит вдруг перед собой:
Владимир, в гриднице высокой,
В кругу седых богатырей,
Между двенадцатью сынами,
С толпою названных гостей   470
Сидит за браными столами.
И так же гневен старый князь,
Как в день ужасный расставанья,
И все сидят не шевелясь,
Не смея перервать молчанья.
Утих веселый шум гостей,

There lay a dale in silence drowsing,   440
enveloped in nocturnal mist;
and through the gloom a fleeting moon
glimmered between the clouds, illuming
with fitful glow a burial mound.
Beneath the mound Ruslán was sitting,
dumb and disconsolate as ever,
beside the comatose princess.
He sat there deep in contemplation,
thoughts swiftly flitting through his head,
while sleep hovered above, unnoticed,   450
and fanned the prince with chilling wings.
Weary, and drowsy now, he turned
with troubled eyes towards the girl,
and, leaning his exhausted head
down at her feet, fell fast asleep.

And it was a portentous sleep:
the warrior seemed to see the princess
standing before a deep abyss,
panic-struck, paralysed and pale…
Then suddenly Lyudmíla vanished,   460
he stood alone above the void…
and from the silent depth there came
a voice he knew, a plaintive call…
He leapt to the princess's aid
and plunged down headlong through the blackness…
Then all at once appeared the Grand Prince
Vladímir in his high-roofed hall,
by grey-haired warrior-lords attended;
he sat at tables richly laid,
his dozen stalwart sons around him   470
and a great gathering of guests.
The agèd prince was just as angry
as on that dreadful day of parting.
All kept their seats; no one dared move,
no one dared interrupt the silence.
No cheerful buzz of company

Не ходит чаша круговая…
И видит он среди гостей
В бою сраженного Рогдая:
Убитый как живой сидит;   480
Из опененного стакана
Он, весел, пьет и не глядит
На изумленного Руслана.
Князь видит и младого хана,
Друзей и недругов… и вдруг
Раздался гуслей беглый звук
И голос вещего Баяна,
Певца героев и забав.
Вступает в гридницу Фарлаф,
Ведет он за руку Людмилу;   490
Но старец, с места не привстав,
Молчит, склонив главу унылу.
Князья, бояре – все молчат,
Душевные движенья кроя.
И всё исчезло – смертный хлад
Объемлет спящего героя.
В дремоту тяжко погружен,
Он льет мучительные слезы,
В волненье мыслит: это сон!
Томится, но зловещей грезы,   500
Увы, прервать не в силах он.

 Луна чуть светит над горою;
Объяты рощи темнотою,
Долина в мертвой тишине…
Изменник едет на коне.
Пред ним открылася поляна;
Он видит сумрачный курган;
У ног Людмилы спит Руслан,
И ходит конь кругом кургана.
Фарлаф с боязнию глядит;   510
В тумане ведьма исчезает,
В нем сердце замерло, дрожит,
Из хладных рук узду роняет,

arose; no loving-cup passed round...
And then he saw among the guests
Rogdáy, whom he had trounced in combat;
though slain, he sat as if alive,   480
and from a foaming mug of beer
drank with a grin, and failed to look
in the amazed Ruslán's direction.
He also saw the youthful khan,
and friends and enemies... and then
a gusli's rippling notes rang out
and the fine voice of skilled Bayán,
singer of fighters and of feasts.
Farláf then strode into the hall,
leading Lyudmíla by the hand;   490
the old Grand Prince, though, made no move;
he let his head hang, sad and silent;
princes and lords stayed silent too,
masking their innermost reactions.
All vanished – and a deadly chill
enwrapped the warrior as he slept.
Sunk deep still in a heavy stupor
he started shedding anguished tears, and
in his distress knew he'd been dreaming;
for all he strove, though, he'd, alas,   500
no strength to shake the nightmare off.

Dim moonlight glimmered on the hills,
the woods stood shrouded deep in darkness,
the dale in deathly silence lay...
the traitor on his steed came riding.
A clearing opened out before him;
he saw the barrow through the gloom,
Ruslán stretched at Lyudmíla's feet,
horse wandering free about the mound.
Farláf peered at the scene in terror;   510
the witch had vanished in the mist;
his heart stood still, then palpitated;
his chilled hands let the bridle fall.

Тихонько обнажает меч,
Готовясь витязя без боя
С размаха надвое рассечь…
К нему подъехал. Конь героя,
Врага почуя, закипел,
Заржал и топнул. Знак напрасный!
Руслан не внемлет; сон ужасный,   520
Как груз, над ним отяготел!…
Изменник, ведьмой ободренный,
Герою в грудь рукой презренной
Вонзает трижды хладну сталь…
И мчится боязливо вдаль
С своей добычей драгоценной.

Всю ночь бесчувственный Руслан
Лежал во мраке под горою.
Часы летели. Кровь рекою
Текла из воспаленных ран.   530
Поутру, взор открыв туманный,
Пуская тяжкий, слабый стон,
С усильем приподнялся он,
Взглянул, поник главою бранной –
И пал недвижный, бездыханный.

Then stealthily he bared his sword,
steeling himself without a fight
to cleave the warrior into two...
He rode up. But the prince's horse,
scenting a foe, reared up at him,
neighed, stamped his fore-hoof. Futile warning!
Ruslán heard nothing; like a deadweight,   520
the dreadful dream pressed down upon him...
Farláf, emboldened by the witch,
into the warrior's chest thrice thrust
his blade's cold steel – a coward's blows!...
then galloped off into the distance
in panic, with his priceless prey.

   All night Ruslán, insensible,
lay in the dark beneath the hill.
The hours flew by. A stream of blood
ran from the warrior's angry wounds.   530
Next morning, opening misty eyes,
and with a feeble, pain-fraught moan,
he forced himself to half-arise,
gazed round, then hung his brave young head,
and fell inert, unbreathing, dead.

ПЕСНЬ ШЕСТАЯ

Ты мне велишь, о друг мой нежный,
На лире легкой и небрежной
Старинны были напевать
И музе верной посвящать
Часы бесценного досуга…
Ты знаешь, милая подруга:
Поссорясь с ветреной молвой,
Твой друг, блаженством упоенный,
Забыл и труд уединенный,
И звуки лиры дорогой.   10
От гармонической забавы
Я, негой упоен, отвык…
Дышу тобой – и гордой славы
Невнятен мне призывный клик!
Меня покинул тайный гений
И вымыслов и сладких дум;
Любовь и жажда наслаждений
Одни преследуют мой ум.
Но ты велишь, но ты любила
Рассказы прежние мои,   20
Преданья славы и любви;
Мой богатырь, моя Людмила,
Владимир, ведьма, Черномор
И Финна верные печали
Твое мечтанье занимали;
Ты, слушая мой легкий вздор,
С улыбкой иногда дремала;
Но иногда свой нежный взор
Нежнее на певца бросала…
Решусь: влюбленный говорун,   30
Касаюсь вновь ленивых струн;

Sixth Canto

It's your choice, gentle friend!* You want me,
amateur minstrel though I am,
to sing again of deeds long past,
and give up the free time we prize
for my old calling as a poet...
As you well know, my darling girl,
in my infatuation with you
I've disavowed my quest for fame
and dropped the lonely work I did
and the word music that I cherished.   10
Drugged with your company, I've ceased
to amuse myself with tuning rhymes...
You are the air I breathe – no longer
do honours or prestige attract me!
Inventiveness, my way with words –
gifts from I know not where – have left me.
Love, and a craving for life's pleasures –
they're all that now preoccupy me.
It's your choice, though; and, truth to tell,
you used to enjoy those tales I told,   20
legends of courage and romance:
Ruslán, Lyudmíla, and Vladímir,
the witch Naína, Chernomór,
the Finn too, ever grave and grieving –
they captured your imagination;
and, as you listened to my nonsense,
sometimes you'd smile a dreamy smile,
or with your gentle eyes you'd look
more gently at me as I read...
Right, then! The doting raconteur,   30
I'll strum once more my idle harp strings;

143

Сажусь у ног твоих и снова
Бренчу про витязя младого.

Но что сказал я? Где Руслан?
Лежит он мертвый в чистом поле:
Уж кровь его не льется боле,
Над ним летает жадный вран,
Безгласен рог, недвижны латы,
Не шевелится шлем косматый!

Вокруг Руслана ходит конь,   40
Поникнув гордой головою,
В его глазах исчез огонь!
Не машет гривой золотою,
Не тешится, не скачет он
И ждет, когда Руслан воспрянет…
Но князя крепок хладный сон,
И долго щит его не грянет.

А Черномор? Он за седлом,
В котомке, ведьмою забытый,
Еще не знает ни о чем;   50
Усталый, сонный и сердитый
Княжну, героя моего
Бранил от скуки молчаливо;
Не слыша долго ничего,
Волшебник выглянул – о диво!
Он видит, богатырь убит;
В крови потопленный лежит;
Людмилы нет, всё пусто в поле;
Злодей от радости дрожит
И мнит: свершилось, я на воле!   60
Но старый карла был неправ.

Меж тем, Наиной осененный,
С Людмилой, тихо усыпленной,
Стремится к Киеву Фарлаф:
Летит, надежды, страха полный;

and, seated at your feet, I'll sing
again to you of young Ruslán.

What's that I said? Where is Ruslán, then?
He's lying in the open, dead,
blood trickling from his wounds no longer,
above, a hungry raven wheeling –
no sound of horn, no stir of armour,
no tremor of his whiskered helm.

Around Ruslán the horse was ambling,   40
hanging the head once held so high,
the sparkle of his eyes extinguished.
He shook his golden mane no more,
he didn't canter, didn't caper,
just waited for Ruslán to wake…
the prince's sleep was cold and deep, though,
and long his shield seemed sure to lie.

And Chernomór? – At rear of saddle,
bagged up, forgotten by Naína,
he didn't know yet what had passed.   50
Tired out, and sleepy, and annoyed,
he killed the time by muttering muted
abuse at prince and princess both.
At last, having for long heard nothing,
the wizard peeped outside. Amazed,
he saw the warrior lying murdered,
surrounded in a pool of blood,
Lyudmíla nowhere, landscape empty.
The villain quivered with delight
and thought: "It's over! Now I'm free!"   60
But the old dwarf was far from right.

Meanwhile, safeguarded by Naína,
Farláf was riding hard for Kiev,
bearing Lyudmíla fast asleep.
He sped on, full of hope and dread;

Пред ним уже днепровски волны
В знакомых пажитях шумят;
Уж видит златоверхий град;
Уже Фарлаф по граду мчится,
И шум на стогнах восстает; 70
В волненье радостном народ
Валит за всадником, теснится;
Бегут обрадовать отца:
И вот изменник у крыльца.

Влача в душе печали бремя,
Владимир-солнышко в то время
В высоком тереме своем
Сидел, томясь привычной думой.
Бояре, витязи кругом
Сидели с важностью угрюмой. 80
Вдруг внемлет он: перед крыльцом
Волненье, крики, шум чудесный;
Дверь отворилась: перед ним
Явился воин неизвестный;
Все встали с шепотом глухим
И вдруг смутились, зашумели:
"Людмила здесь! Фарлаф… ужели?"
В лице печальном изменясь,
Встает со стула старый князь,
Спешит тяжелыми шагами 90
К несчастной дочери своей,
Подходит; отчими руками
Он хочет прикоснуться к ней;
Но дева милая не внемлет
И очарованная дремлет
В руках убийцы – все глядят
На князя в смутном ожиданье;
И старец беспокойный взгляд
Вперил на витязя в молчанье.
Но, хитро перст к устам прижав, 100
"Людмила спит, – сказал Фарлаф, –
Я так нашел ее недавно

soon he espied the Dnieper's waters
lapping the fields he knew so well;
soon he discerned the gold-domed city;
soon he was pounding down its streets,
horse's hoofs clattering on the stones.   70
Behind Farláf excited throngs
of happy townsfolk surged and jostled;
they ran to bring the father joy...
and now the traitor's at the steps!

   Bowed by his inner load of sorrow,
meanwhile, Vladímir the Resplendent*
was sitting in his high-roofed hall,
racked with anxiety unending.
In grim solemnity around him
were seated noblemen and knights.   80
He heard a sudden noise: outside
commotion, cries, unwonted uproar.
The door burst open, and in strode
a knight he didn't recognize;
the guests rose with a muffled murmur;
then sudden tumult, pandemonium:
"Lyudmíla's here! Farláf? – it can't be!"
The glum face of the Grand Prince brightened;
the old man got up from his chair
and hobbled, stiff but with all haste,   90
to welcome back his hapless daughter.
He came up close, and made as if
to clasp her in a father's arms;
but the beloved girl lay senseless,
held by the murderer, still sleeping
under the magic spell; the guests
watched the Grand Prince confused, expectant.
The agèd father fixed his gaze,
wordless and anxious, on Farláf,
who pressed a finger to his lips   100
slyly and said: "Lyudmíla's sleeping.
I found her like this not long back

147

В пустынных муромских лесах
У злого лешего в руках;
Там совершилось дело славно;
Три дня мы билися; луна
Над боем трижды подымалась;
Он пал, а юная княжна
Мне в руки сонною досталась;
И кто прервет сей дивный сон?   110
Когда настанет пробужденье?
Не знаю – скрыт судьбы закон!
А нам надежда и терпенье
Одни остались в утешенье".

И вскоре с вестью роковой
Молва по граду полетела;
Народа пестрою толпой
Градская площадь закипела;
Печальный терем всем открыт;
Толпа волнуется, валит   120
Туда, где на одре высоком,
На одеяле парчевом
Княжна лежит во сне глубоком
Князья и витязи кругом
Стоят унылы; гласы трубны,
Рога, тимпаны, гусли, бубны
Гремят над нею; старый князь,
Тоской тяжелой изнурясь,
К ногам Людмилы сединами
Приник с безмолвными слезами;   130
И бледный близ него Фарлаф,
В немом раскаянье, в досаде
Трепещет, дерзость потеряв.

Настала ночь. Никто во граде
Очей бессонных не смыкал;
Шумя, теснились все друг к другу:
О чуде всякий толковал;
Младой супруг свою супругу

in empty forests Múrom-way,*
the captive of an evil wood sprite.*
The whole affair went splendidly;
we fought for three whole days; the moon
rose three times on our savage combat;
the wood sprite fell; the young princess, though,
once rescued, proved to be asleep.
And who can break her magic slumber?   110
When will her time of waking come?
Heaven alone knows that – not I.
Patience and hope – they're all the comfort
left us at this distressing time."

   The fateful news had very soon
spread through the town by word of mouth.
A heaving throng from every class
converged upon the city square;
the mournful chamber's doors stood open.
The crowd surged forward, agitated,   120
till they could see the princess lying
asleep upon a lofty bier
on draperies of rich brocade;
around her princes, knights were standing
downcast; and from a gallery
horns, trumpets, gusli, drums and cymbals
played deafeningly. The old Grand Prince,
worn out with sorrow and vexation,
bowed his grey head in voiceless tears
at his dear princess-daughter's feet.   130
Near to him, pallid-faced, Farláf,
in mute remorse and self-disgust,
stood trembling, his bravado gone.

   Night fell; but no one in the city
could close their wakeful eyes in sleep;
they huddled noisily in groups,
all talking of the strange event;
even young husbands left their wives

149

В светлице скромной забывал.
Но только свет луны двурогой   140
Исчез пред утренней зарей,
Весь Киев новою тревогой
Смутился! Клики, шум и вой
Возникли всюду. Киевляне
Толпятся на стене градской…
И видят: в утреннем тумане
Шатры белеют за рекой;
Щиты, как зарево, блистают,
В полях наездники мелькают,
Вдали подъемля черный прах;   150
Идут походные телеги,
Костры пылают на холмах.
Беда: восстали печенеги!

Но в это время вещий Финн,
Духов могучий властелин,
В своей пустыне безмятежной,
С спокойным сердцем ожидал,
Чтоб день судьбины неизбежной,
Давно предвиденный, восстал.

В немой глуши степей горючих,   160
За дальной цепью диких гор,
Жилища ветров, бурь гремучих,
Куда и ведьмы смелый взор
Проникнуть в поздний час боится,
Долина чудная таится,
И в той долине два ключа:
Один течет волной *живою*,
По камням весело журча,
Тот льется *мертвою* водою;
Кругом всё тихо, ветры спят,   170
Прохлада вешняя не веет,
Столетни сосны не шумят,
Не вьются птицы, лань не смеет
В жар летний пить из тайных вод;

alone and chaste in nuptial bedrooms.
The new moon, though, had hardly yet   140
been dimmed by morning's early glow,
when all of Kiev was disturbed
by further trouble. Shouts, yells, hubbub
arose on every side. Kievans
were gathering on the city walls...
There in the morning mist they saw
across the river white tents gleaming,
shields flashing red like shafts of dawn,
armed horsemen glinting on the grasslands
and kicking up dark clouds of dust.   150
Wagons of war were trundling closer;
along the hillsides campfires blazed – yes,
trouble: a Pecheneg* invasion!

Throughout this time the wise old Finn,
dread master of the spirit world,
in his retreat remote and lonely,
had waited, unperturbed at heart,
for the arrival of the day
so long foreseen, so surely fixed.

Beyond a chain of distant crags,   160
abode of gales and howling storms,
stretch soundless wastes of scorching steppe
where even witches' brazen eyes
fear in the night to penetrate.
There lies a strange and secret valley,
and in that valley rise two springs.
One of them gushes *living* water,
which gurgles gaily around the rocks.
The second spring sends forth *dead* water:
all round is silence; no wind stirs;   170
no breath of springtime cools the air;
no age-old pines sigh in the stillness;
no bird flies there; no doe in summer
dares drink from out that baleful pool.

151

Чета духов с начала мира,
Безмолвная на лоне мира,
Дремучий берег стережет…
С двумя кувшинами пустыми
Предстал отшельник перед ними;
Прервали духи давний сон   180
И удалились, страха полны.
Склонившись, погружает он
Сосуды в девственные волны;
Наполнил, в воздухе пропал
И очутился в два мгновенья
В долине, где Руслан лежал
В крови, безгласный, без движенья;
И стал над рыцарем старик,
И вспрыснул мертвою водою,
И раны засияли вмиг,   190
И труп чудесной красотою
Процвел; тогда водой живою
Героя старец окропил,
И бодрый, полный новых сил,
Трепеща жизнью молодою,
Встает Руслан, на ясный день
Очами жадными взирает;
Как безобразный сон, как тень,
Пред ним минувшее мелькает.
Но где Людмила? Он один!   200
В нем сердце, вспыхнув, замирает.
Вдруг витязь вспрянул; вещий Финн
Его зовет и обнимает:
"Судьба свершилась, о мой сын!
Тебя блаженство ожидает;
Тебя зовет кровавый пир;
Твой грозный меч бедою грянет;
На Киев снидет кроткий мир,
И там она тебе предстанет.
Возьми заветное кольцо,   210
Коснися им чела Людмилы,
И тайных чар исчезнут силы,

From the beginning of the world
two spirits, dumb and undisturbed, had
guarded those waters' tangled verges...
Now, when the hermit-Finn appeared
bearing a pair of empty pitchers,
the two cut short their age-long dreams   180
and sped away in high alarm.
The Finn stooped down and dipped his jars
into each virgin spring in turn;
he filled them, then evaporated,
and in two instants reappeared in
the dale in which Ruslán still lay
bloodied, unspeaking and unstirring.
The old man stood above the knight
and sprinkled the dead water on him;
at once his scars grew smooth again,   190
and the dead body bloomed with beauty,
a wondrous beauty. Then the sage
shook living water on the warrior:
in health again, his strength renewed,
young vigour stirring fresh within him,
Ruslán stood up, and at the daylight
gazed with eyes hungering for more.
Like a dark, ugly dream the past
flashed for a moment through his mind –
where was Lyudmíla, though? He'd lost her!   200
His heart glowed hot within, then failed;
he started forward; but the Finn,
feelingly, called him and embraced him:
"What had to be has been, my son!
Good fortune's now awaiting you.
You're summoned to a feast of blood,
where your dread sword will spread destruction.
Peace and goodwill will come to Kiev;
and there you'll find the wife you love.
Now take from me this sacred ring,   210
and with it touch Lyudmíla's forehead:
the dark spell's power will then be broken,

Врагов смутит твое лицо,
Настанет мир, погибнет злоба.
Достойны счастья будьте оба!
Прости надолго, витязь мой!
Дай руку… там, за дверью гроба –
Не прежде – свидимся с тобой!"
Сказал, исчезнул. Упоенный
Восторгом пылким и немым,   220
Руслан, для жизни пробужденный,
Подъемлет руки вслед за ним.
Но ничего не слышно боле!
Руслан один в пустынном поле;
Запрыгав, с карлой за седлом,
Русланов конь нетерпеливый
Бежит и ржет, махая гривой;
Уж князь готов, уж он верхом,
Уж он летит живой и здравый
Через поля, через дубравы.   230

    Но между тем какой позор
Являет Киев осажденный?
Там, устремив на нивы взор,
Народ, уньем пораженный,
Стоит на башнях и стенах
И в страхе ждет небесной казни;
Стенанья робкие в домах,
На стогнах тишина боязни;
Один, близ дочери своей,
Владимир в горестной молитве;   240
И храбрый сонм богатырей
С дружиной верною князей
Готовится к кровавой битве.

    И день настал. Толпы врагов
С зарею двинулись с холмов;
Неукротимые дружины,
Волнуясь, хлынули с равнины
И потекли к стене градской;

and you'll confound your enemies,
peace will prevail, and malice founder.
Deserve your bliss, then, both of you!
Farewell for long, my warrior friend!
Shake hands... It's now beyond death's doorway –
not sooner – that we'll meet again!"
He spoke, and vanished. Overcome
by emotions he could not express,   220
Ruslán, awake now to the world,
held out his hands towards the Finn...
but there were no more words to hear,
no one in that wild dale but him!
His stallion reared impatiently,
the dwarf still there behind the saddle;
he cantered, whinnied, tossed his mane.
Ruslán was ready now, was mounted,
was galloping through wooded hills
and open plains, alive and strong.   230

  Meanwhile, though, what a sorry scene
Kiev presented under siege!
The townsfolk, shattered and despairing,
were standing on the towers and walls,
staring at the surrounding fields and
waiting in terror for their doom;
in every home were muffled moans,
on every street a hush of fear.
Alone now by his daughter's side,
Vladímir stood in anguished prayer.   240
The brave battalion of his warlords,
joined by the loyal princely lifeguard,
made ready for the bloody fray.

  A new day came. Hordes of invaders
at first light moved down off the hills;
unruly companies of fighters
surging in waves across the low ground
hurled themselves at the city walls.

Во граде трубы загремели,
Бойцы сомкнулись, полетели 250
Навстречу рати удалой,
Сошлись – и заварился бой.
Почуя смерть, взыграли кони,
Пошли стучать мечи о брони;
Со свистом туча стрел взвилась,
Равнина кровью залилась;
Стремглав наездники помчались,
Дружины конные смешались;
Сомкнутой, дружною стеной
Там рубится со строем строй; 260
Со всадником там пеший бьется.
Там конь испуганный несется;
Там клики битвы, там побег;
Там русский пал, там печенег;
Тот опрокинут булавою;
Тот легкой поражен стрелою;
Другой, придавленный щитом,
Растоптан бешеным конем…
И длился бой до темной ночи;
Ни враг, ни наш не одолел! 270
За грудами кровавых тел
Бойцы сомкнули томны очи,
И крепок был их бранный сон;
Лишь изредка на поле битвы
Был слышен падших скорбный стон
И русских витязей молитвы.

Бледнела утренняя тень,
Волна сребрилася в потоке,
Сомнительный рождался день
На отуманенном востоке. 280
Яснели холмы и леса,
И просыпались небеса.
Еще в бездейственном покое
Дремало поле боевое;
Вдруг сон прервался: вражий стан

Within the city bugles blared,
soldiers in tight formation sallied   250
out to confront the reckless foe,
engaged with them – and battle raged.
Warhorses scenting death, exultant,
raced to strike sword against cuirass;
dark clouds of arrows hissed and whistled;
the battlefield was drenched with blood;
riders rushed headlong into combat,
whole mounted squadrons clashed and scuffled.
Here lines of troops, like human walls,
close-formed, were butchering each other;   260
there a foot soldier fought a horseman;
elsewhere a horse ran wild with fright;
Pechenegs, Russians, both were dying;
here battle cries, there men in flight.
One warrior had been clubbed to death,
an arrow had transfixed another;
one other, crushed beneath his shield,
lay trampled by a frenzied horse...
The conflict carried on till nightfall;
no side had won the upper hand.   270
Behind great heaps of gruesome corpses
soldiers lay down and closed their eyes.
Deeply the battle-weary slept;
just now and then across the field
you'd hear the dying groan with pain
and Russian warriors' voices praying.

The early morning's gloom was thinning;
and on the Dnieper silver gleamed;
a doubtful day began to glimmer
across the misty eastern skies.   280
Forests and hills were showing clearer,
from heavy torpor heaven awoke.
The battlefield was slumbering still
in calm and inactivity,
when at an instant sleep was shattered

С тревогой шумною воспрянул,
Внезапный крик сражений грянул;
Смутилось сердце киевлян;
Бегут нестройными толпами
И видят: в поле меж врагами,   290
Блистая в латах, как в огне,
Чудесный воин на коне
Грозой несется, колет, рубит,
В ревущий рог, летая, трубит...
То был Руслан. Как божий гром,
Наш витязь пал на басурмана;
Он рыщет с карлой за седлом
Среди испуганного стана.
Где ни просвищет грозный меч,
Где конь сердитый ни промчится,   300
Везде главы слетают с плеч
И с воплем строй на строй валится;
В одно мгновенье бранный луг
Покрыт холмами тел кровавых,
Живых, раздавленных, безглавых,
Громадой копий, стрел, кольчуг.

    На трубный звук, на голос боя
Дружины конные славян
Помчались по следам героя,
Сразились... гибни, басурман!   310
Объемлет ужас печенегов;
Питомцы бурные набегов
Зовут рассеянных коней,
Противиться не смеют боле
И с диким воплем в пыльном поле
Бегут от киевских мечей,
Обречены на жертву аду;
Их сонмы русский меч казнит;
Ликует Киев... Но по граду
Могучий богатырь летит;   320
В деснице держит меч победный;
Копье сияет как звезда;

by uproar in the opposing camp
and by an unexpected war cry.
The Kievans, alarmed, confused,
ran out in crowds without formation
to look: out there amid the foe,   290
in armour shimmering like flame,
a superhuman warrior, mounted,
was charging storm-like, cleaving, slashing,
blasting his horn as he advanced...
Ruslán it was: like heaven's lightning,
he fell upon the heathen horde,
careering through their terrified
encampment, dwarf still bagged behind him.
Wherever raced the furious stallion,
wherever whistled that dread sword,   300
everywhere heads were lopped from shoulders,
and rank fell back on rank with screams.
In moments was the field of battle
bestrewn with mounds of bloodied men –
some still alive, some smashed, some headless –
and heaps of arrows, spears and mail.

Hearing the blast of horn and war cry,
the Slavic horsemen in their squadrons
galloped to aid their champion,
joined battle – and vowed "Death to heathens!"   310
The Pechenegs were gripped with terror;
those savage raiders born and bred
were rounding up their scattered steeds now;
they'd no more stomach for the fight;
and, yelling wildly through the dust,
they ran to escape the Kiev swordsmen,
hell's destined victims though they were.
The Russians crushed the horde that day;
and Kiev cheered... But the triumphant
fighter-prince flew across the city.   320
His hand still grasped the victor's sword,
his lance-head glinted like a star,

Струится кровь с кольчуги медной;
На шлеме вьется борода;
Летит, надеждой окрыленный,
По стогнам шумным в княжий дом.
Народ, восторгом упоенный,
Толпится с кликами кругом,
И князя радость оживила.

В безмолвный терем входит он,   330
Где дремлет чудным сном Людмила;
Владимир, в думу погружен,
У ног ее стоял унылый.
Он был один. Его друзей
Война влекла в поля кровавы.
Но с ним Фарлаф, чуждаясь славы,
Вдали от вражеских мечей,
В душе презрев тревоги стана,
Стоял на страже у дверей.
Едва злодей узнал Руслана,   340
В нем кровь остыла, взор погас,
В устах открытых замер глас,
И пал без чувств он на колена…
Достойной казни ждет измена!
Но, помня тайный дар кольца,
Руслан летит к Людмиле спящей,
Ее спокойного лица
Касается рукой дрожащей…
И чудо: юная княжна,
Вздохнув, открыла светлы очи!   350
Казалось, будто бы она
Дивилася столь долгой ночи;
Казалось, что какой-то сон
Ее томил мечтой неясной,
И вдруг узнала – это он!
И князь в объятиях прекрасной.
Воскреснув пламенной душой,
Руслан не видит, не внимает,
И старец в радости немой,
Рыдая, милых обнимает.   360

blood trickled from his bronze cuirass,
the beard still fluttered from his helmet.
He flew on, borne by wings of hope,
through streets and squares to princely palace.
Townsfolk, excited and elated,
thronged round him, shouting words of welcome;
their jubilance gave him new heart.

Ruslán entered the silent hall;   330
Lyudmíla lay there slumbering, spellbound;
Vladímir, steeped in contemplation,
stood at her feet in deep despair,
alone – his courtier-comrades having
answered the call to war and carnage.
Farláf was there, though, shunning notice;
he loathed the stress and strain of camp;
so, out of range of hostile swordsmen,
he stood watch at the palace doors.
Once the wretch recognized Ruslán,   340
his blood ran cold, his eyes grew dim,
his voice died on his open lips –
he fell insensate to his knees,
awaiting a betrayer's death.
The magic ring, though, filled Ruslán's thoughts;
he flew to where the princess slept.
Holding outstretched a hand that trembled
he let it touch her tranquil face…
A miracle! Lyudmíla murmured,
opened those radiant eyes of hers –   350
full of surprise she seemed to be
to waken from so long a night;
but disconcerted too she seemed
by an obscure and troubling dream.
And then she realized: there he was! –
and clasped her husband in her arms…
Restored to life, his heart aflame,
Ruslán had eyes and ears for nothing;
and old Vladímir, speechless, sobbing
for joy, embraced the loving pair.   360

Чем кончу длинный мой рассказ?
Ты угадаешь, друг мой милый!
Неправый старца гнев погас;
Фарлаф пред ним и пред Людмилой
У ног Руслана объявил
Свой стыд и мрачное злодейство;
Счастливый князь ему простил;
Лишенный силы чародейства,
Был принят карла во дворец;
И, бедствий празднуя конец,   370
Владимир в гриднице высокой
Запировал в семье своей.

Дела давно минувших дней,
Преданья старины глубокой.

How shall I end my lengthy tale?
Not hard for you to guess, my dear!
Quenched was Vladímir's wrongful wrath.
He and Lyudmíla watched Farláf
grovel before Ruslán, avowing
with shame his dark and evil deeds;
elated still, Ruslán forgave him.
The dwarf, his magic power now lost,
was kept on in the princely household.
To mark the end of grief and woe,   370
Vladímir in his high-roofed hall
held a great feast for one and all.

A tale of the times of old!
The deeds of days of other years!*

ЭПИЛОГ

Так, мира житель равнодушный,
На лоне праздной тишины,
Я славил лирою послушной
Преданья темной старины.
Я пел – и забывал обиды
Слепого счастья и врагов,
Измены ветреной Дориды
И сплетни шумные глупцов.
На крыльях вымысла носимый,
Ум улетал за край земной;   10
И между тем грозы незримой
Сбиралась туча надо мной!…
Я погибал… Святой хранитель
Первоначальных, бурных дней,
О дружба, нежный утешитель
Болезненной души моей!
Ты умолила непогоду;
Ты сердцу возвратила мир;
Ты сохранила мне свободу,
Кипящей младости кумир!   20

Забытый светом и молвою,
Далече от брегов Невы,
Теперь я вижу пред собою
Кавказа гордые главы.
Над их вершинами крутыми,
На скате каменных стремнин,
Питаюсь чувствами немыми
И чудной прелестью картин
Природы дикой и угрюмой;
Душа, как прежде, каждый час   30
Полна томительною думой –

Epilogue*

So – carefree, cosmopolitan,
at ease, at leisure, and at peace,
there was I glibly celebrating
the sombre legends of our past.
Engrossed in verse, I paid no heed to
the spite of blind ill luck and foes,
the bad faith of a fickle girlfriend,*
and the shrill chattering of fools.
Borne up on wings of fantasy,
my mind soared off beyond this earth, 10
while meantime thunderclouds, unnoticed,
were massing thickly overhead!...
I would have perished... But, friends, bless you,
you rescued me in those first days
just as the tempest broke; your kindness
brought me relief in my distress.
By your appeals the storm was stilled;
you gave me back my peace of mind;
saved me my freedom – precious icon
to an impetuous lad like me! 20

Now, far from the Nevá's* embankments,
dismissed from salon talk and minds,
I'm standing awe-struck – there before me
the soaring peaks of Caucasus.
High on their dizzying precipices,
where rocky gorges yawn below,
I'm drawing sustenance from feelings
I can't express, and from the breathless
beauty of vistas wild and harsh.
Within me, hour by hour, as ever, 30
I'm tantalized by thoughts aplenty –

Но огнь поэзии погас.
Ищу напрасно впечатлений:
Она прошла, пора стихов,
Пора любви, веселых снов,
Пора сердечных вдохновений!
Восторгов краткий день протек –
И скрылась от меня навек
Богиня тихих песнопений…

but my poetic fire is spent.
I seek in vain for stimulation:
passed is my time of versifying,
my time of love, of joyful dreams,
my time of unforced inspiration.
My ecstasy's brief day's no more –
she whom I hymned in veneration
is lost to me for evermore…*

Note on the Text

The Russian text of this edition follows closely the standard text published in Russia (see bibliography), which is based on the second edition published in Pushkin's lifetime, that of 1828. I have, however, also consulted directly both the 1828 text and that of the first edition published in 1820.

Notes and Commentary

p. 5, *Prologue*: The Prologue, a particularly limpid, graceful and evocative piece of writing, has over time become more famous than *Ruslan and Lyudmila* itself. It presents a crowded tapestry of themes from Russian folklore (where the details of particular stories are somewhat fluid and interchangeable).

There was no prologue to the first edition of the poem in 1820. Pushkin wrote the piece probably in late 1824, when he was living under restriction in the country and making notes (which still survive) of Russian fairy tales told him by his old nurse Arína Rodionovna Yákovleva (1758–1828). Several of the motifs from the nurse's tales are included in the piece; Pushkin may well have written it initially to introduce a worked-up version of one of them, though in the event he did not write the tales up till the next decade. In the meantime he made use of this introductory piece as a prologue to the 1828 edition of *Ruslan and Lyudmila*, where it is printed at the opening of Canto I.

The prologue contains nothing to link it to *Ruslan and Lyudmila* more than to another fairy story. Moreover, its attribution of the story that follows to a "learnèd cat" is at variance with Pushkin's (playful) suggestion in the body of the poem (Canto V, ll. 225–28) that it came from a monastic chronicler.

Details about the elements of Russian folklore alluded to in the prologue follow:

The fabulous *oak*, the *chain of gold*, the *learnèd cat* who *sings songs* and *tells fairy tales* (lines 1–6) figure in a tale told by Pushkin's nurse that formed the basis of his *Tale of Tsar Saltán*.

The *wood sprite* (*léshy* – line 7) was a figure of Russian folklore, part-animal, part-goblin; he was a mischievous and often dangerous denizen of the Russian forest, personifying its nature as a sinister place hostile to humans. Pushkin mentions a *léshy* in Canto VI, ll. 104–09.

Rusálkas (line 8) were water-spirits of Slavic folklore, something like the undines and mermaids of Western Europe. They normally took the form of attractive young girls, naked or lightly clad, and were believed to embody the souls of drowned virgins. They lived for the most part beneath the surface of rivers and lakes, but at certain times they emerged at night and climbed into riverside willows or birches, where they might be seen combing their hair. They took pleasure in luring men to their patch of water and then dragging them down into the depths. They appear a couple of times in *Ruslan and Lyudmila* – Canto II, l. 496 and Canto IV, l. 214.

The *hut… on chicken's legs* (lines 11, 12), which could thereby turn around or move about, was traditionally the home of the witch Bába-Yagá – see below.

The *thirty champions* that emerge from the sea attended by an old man (lines 15–17) is another motif that Pushkin took from a folk tale told him by his nurse, on which he later based his *Tale of Tsar Saltán*. In his own version Pushkin tells again of the ocean waves rolling in across empty sands, and thirty *three* armed warriors, fine young men, emerging onto the beach with their tutor (there named Chernomór). Thirty, or thirty three, are frequent numbers for a troop of warriors or other groups in Russian folklore.

The *king's son* who *takes prisoner an awesome tsar* (lines 18, 19) seems to come from the popular story of *Bová the king's son* (on which Pushkin at school commenced a light-hearted narrative poem), which contains episodes of this kind.

The *wizard* who *hauls a warrior brave* up in the sky above woods and waves (lines 20–22) is a traditional fairy-tale motif which Pushkin had already incorporated into the storyline of *Ruslan and Lyudmila* – see Canto V, ll. 53–97.

The *princess* in a dungeon with a *brown-haired wolf* (lines 23, 24): Pushkin seems to have adapted a folklore motif (which features, for instance, in one of the Firebird tales) about a persecuted *prince* loyally supported by a *grey* wolf.

A mortar in a witch's form (lines 25, 26): Pushkin names the witch Bába-Yagá (which in its English form does not fit easily into an iambic line!). In Russian folklore Bába-Yagá was a hideous and fearsome witch who lived in a hut that stood on hen's legs (see above); when she flew over the earth in the form of an iron mortar, she caused storms, plagues and general distress, and anyone seeing her was struck dumb.

Kashchéy (line 27) (sometimes spelt "Koshchéy") was traditionally a malevolent wizard who hoarded treasures and was immune to death. He was also known as a cannibal, who seized young girls and carried them off to his kingdom. The only way to kill Kashchéy was to crush a certain egg, which would be found in a duck, which would be found in a hare, which would be found in an iron chest, which was buried at the foot of a green oak tree by the sea on the island of Buyán. Pushkin's old nurse had told him a tale about Tsar Kashchéy, in which Kashchéy refused to let his daughter marry while he remained alive. His daughter, in desperation, traced the secret of her father's deathlessness to the egg, which she secured for herself, whereupon Kashchéy began to sicken. Tsar Kashchéy figures in the firebird folk tale on which Stravinsky based his *Firebird* ballet as the possessive owner of the magic garden in which the firebird dwells.

Rus (line 28) is an archaic form of "Russia", mostly used of the Russia, legendary and historical, of the Kiev period (from the tenth to the thirteenth centuries AD).

p. 9, *A tale... of other years!*: Pushkin opened the First Canto and closed the Sixth (Canto VI, ll. 373, 374) – in the first edition the beginning and end of the whole poem – with these two lines from Ossian in Russian translation.

Ossian, son of Fingal, was a figure from Celtic legend: in youth a mighty warrior, he became in later life a blind minstrel who composed and sang poetry about the exploits of the Celtic kings and warriors of Ireland and Scotland. In the 1760s James Macpherson (1736–96), a Scotsman, published a collection of what he claimed were English translations of Gaelic poetry he had transcribed in the Highlands from traditional ballad-singers and storytellers. He presented this collection as fragments of long-lost epic poems by Ossian, dating back to the early centuries of our era. The poems, with their apparent antiquity and distinctive Celtic background, caused a sensation both in Britain and, after translation into French and other European languages, across literary Europe; they exercised a major influence on the development of the romantic movement. Not many years later, however, the whole collection was denounced, by Dr Johnson among others, as a literary fraud – a charge that Macpherson was never able convincingly to refute.

The Ossianic poems continued, however, to influence European culture into the nineteenth century. They evoke a long-lost world located (like the world of *Ruslan and Lyudmila*) on the borders between legend and history and between paganism and Christianity. Pushkin himself, as a schoolboy in 1814, had composed some Russian adaptations of Ossianic poetry. The lines he used at the beginning and end of *Ruslan and Lyudmila* come from the beginning of "Ossian's" *Carthon*, where they are repeated a paragraph later, like a minstrel's refrain. Pushkin seems to have chosen them to set the atmosphere of a tale handed down over the centuries by epic minstrels, like the epic ballads of Russia (*bylíny*).

In translating these two lines back to English, I have used the original words of the Ossianic poem, which happen almost to fit Pushkin's metre.

p. 9, *Grand Prince Vladímir the Resplendent*: Literally "Vladímir the Sun", a title commonly given to the legendary Grand Prince of Kiev in the traditional Russian epic ballads, or *bylíny*. Collections of these ballads in written form had already been published in Russia by the time Pushkin was working on *Ruslan and Lyudmila*. The ballads portray Vladímir as a senior and respected ruler in a superficially Christianized court, peopled by heroes of superhuman stature and powers, who were forever going out to battle with mythical beasts and pagan "tatars"; Vladímir was much given to lengthy feasting and mead-drinking with his princes, nobles, warriors and wealthy guests, to the accompaniment of gusli-playing minstrels.

This legendary monarch reflects a historical figure. Vladímir I, Grand Prince of Kiev from about 980 to 1015, was one of the greatest rulers of Kievan Rus, the land of the eastern Slavs centred on Kiev, which covered much of what is now Ukraine and western Russia, and reached its zenith in the eleventh and early twelfth centuries AD. After an early attempt to establish a form of paganism as the religion of the country, Vladímir in 988 adopted Christianity both for himself and for his nation; he was later canonized as Saint Vladímir. The historical Vladímir had a large family, including at least twelve sons.

Vladímir's reign was remembered as a golden age of strength, prosperity and culture for Kiev. He was a generous ruler, building churches and providing lavish hospitality. Karamzín, whose great historical work covering that period came out as Pushkin was starting work on *Ruslan and Lyudmila*, records on the authority of contemporary monastic chronicles that, to celebrate one victory over his troublesome pagan neighbours the Pechenegs, Vladímir held an eight-day feast with his nobles, for which he ordered the brewing of 300 barrels of mead. Thereafter Vladímir provided a weekly feast "in his high-roofed... hall" in Kiev (Pushkin uses the same rare word for "hall" as Karamzín) for his nobles, officers and leading citizens; he also allowed the poor of the city to come to his palace for food and financial assistance, and arranged distributions of food and drink through the city for those who were too ill to come in person. He was notably humane in other ways too, fostering where possible peaceful relations with his neighbours and for a while commuting the death penalty, even for murder, to a fine.

For his picture of Kiev under Vladímir in the early lines of the First Canto and the latter part of the Sixth, Pushkin drew both on the traditional ballads and on Karamzín's history. In his references to warfare and armour he clearly followed Karamzín's account of these in the Kiev period. He played down Vladímir's adoption of Christianity, however, no doubt because at this period of his life he had little interest in religion and because mention of Christian practices would have sat ill with the wizardry of much of the story.

p. 9, *gusli's*: A gusli was a traditional Russian instrument of the zither family with a harplike sound, used by minstrels to accompany their ballads.

p. 9, *Bayán*: Bayán is mentioned in the ancient Russian epic *The Lay of Igor's Host* (*c.*1186) as a minstrel with magic powers who lived in the time of Vladímir I.

p. 11, *Khazar*: In the eighth and ninth centuries Khazaria had been a powerful state, ruled by kagans or khans, centred to the north of the Caspian Sea; it was an eastern neighbour and rival to Kievan Rus. It included peoples of a variety of races and faiths, but the ruling class are said to have adopted Judaism as their religion. In 965 AD the Khazars' power was destroyed by Vladímir's father Svyatosláv and their lands were subsequently engulfed by the Pechenegs and other marauding tribes from the east.

p. 17, *Dnieper's*: The Dnieper, on which Kiev stands, is one of the major rivers of eastern Europe, rising in the Central Russian Uplands and flowing south through Belarus and Ukraine till it eventually issues into the Black Sea.

p. 23, *Finnish-born*: Finnish-speaking peoples were once much more widely spread than now across northern Russia. The historian Karamzín, whom Pushkin had just read when composing *Ruslan and Lyudmila*, mentions that in early Scandinavia and in Russia the Finns were noted for their use of magic. Witch doctors (shamans) did indeed feature prominently in the pre-Christian religion of the Finnish-speaking peoples.

p. 28, *Герой… тебя*: Pushkin dropped six lines from the 1820 edition here – see Appendix, item A.

p. 30, *В мечтах… лесной*: Pushkin shortened the 1820 text by four lines here – see Appendix, item B.

p. 38, *Сердиться… грешно*: Pushkin dropped four lines from the 1820 edition here – see Appendix, item C.

p. 50, *Людмила… светлица*: Pushkin dropped two lines from the 1820 edition here – see Appendix, item D.

p. 50, *Три девы… подошли*: Pushkin shortened the 1820 text by eight lines here – see Appendix, item E.

p. 51, *Scheherazade*: Scheherazade (or Shahrazad) was the heroine of the frame story for a cycle of Arabic tales known as *A Thousand and One Nights*, which includes such tales as Aladdin, Ali Baba, and Sinbad the Sailor. The frame story tells how Scheherazade, newly married to a king who killed each of his wives on the first night of their marriage, deferred her own execution night after night by beginning an exotic story of love, magic, adventure or suchlike one evening and refusing to finish it till the next. After a thousand and one nights the king, enchanted by the stories, agreed to lift the death sentence.

p. 55, *Armida's*: Armida was a sorceress in the 1581 poem *Gerusalemme liberata* by Torquato Tasso (1544–95); her enchanted garden is described in its 16th canto.

p. 55, *King Solomon*: In the Old Testament Book of *Ecclesiastes*, traditionally ascribed to King Solomon (King of Israel, *c.*961–922 BC), the writer says: "I made myself gardens and parks, and planted in them all kinds of fruit trees. I made myself pools from which to water the forest of growing trees." (*Ecclesiastes* 2:5,6). Gardens, and imagery drawn from gardens, also figure prominently in the *Song of Solomon* – e.g. 5:1, 6:2.

p. 55, *Prince Potyómkin*: "Prince of Tauris" in the original. Grigóry Alexándrovich Potyómkin (1739–91), Russian courtier, general and administrator, favourite and lover of Catherine the Great (reigned 1762–96), was given the title of Prince of Tauris by the Empress after his conquest of the Crimea (anciently "Tauris").

In further recognition of this and other services, Catherine built Potyómkin the magnificent Tauride Palace in St Petersburg with extensive landscaped gardens. Adjoining the Palace (which still exists) there was also a huge covered winter garden, the biggest in Europe, equipped with an immense system of hot-water pipes and flues and stocked with exotic plants, so that even in the winter cold of St Petersburg Potyómkin and his guests could stroll in a Mediterranean environment. Simon Sebag-Montefiore quotes the following description on page 468 of his *Prince of Princes – a Life of Potemkin* (Weidenfeld and Nicolson, 2000): "The huge glass hall was supported by columns in the form of palm trees which contained warm water pipes. [It was] an organized jungle of exotic plants, 'flowers, hyacinths and narcissuses, myrtles, orange trees in plenty' – where the walls were all mirrors that concealed more immense stoves. Lamps and diamonds were hidden in mock bunches of grapes, clusters of pears and pineapples so that everything seemed alight... The cupola was painted like the sky. Paths and little hillocks criss-crossed this arbour, leading to statues of goddesses. Its most striking effect was its 'infinite perspective', for Catherine could see straight through the brightness of the Colonnade Hall into the tropical lightness of the Winter Garden and, further, through its glass walls into the English Garden outside, where its 'sanded paths wind, hills rise up, valleys fall away, cuttings open groves, ponds sparkle'..." The parallels with Chernomór's magic garden are notable.

p. 55, *Pheidias* (fifth century BC) was the most renowned of the sculptors of classical Greece. Among other works he designed sculptures for the Parthenon in Athens, including the sculptured reliefs, remains of which (the "Elgin Marbles") are now in the British Museum in London.

p. 55, *protégé of Art's patron gods*: Pushkin refers to "the protégé of Phoebus [Apollo] and Pallas [Athene]": Apollo and Athene were patron deities of arts and crafts in ancient Greece.

p. 56, *Повсюду... тропам*: Pushkin shortened the 1820 text by three lines here – see Appendix, item F.

p. 56, *И дале... путь*: Pushkin dropped eight lines from the 1820 edition here – see Appendix, item G.

p. 63, *Orlóvsky*: Alexander O Orlóvsky (1777–1832) was a contemporary artist who specialized in drawing scenes of combat, particularly on horseback.

p. 65, *rusalka*: See under note on the Prologue.

p. 67, *Zoïlus*: Zoïlus was a Greek orator, cynic philosopher and literary critic of the fourth century BC noted for his bitter attacks on established writers, notably Homer. His nine-book treatise on Homer criticized such aspects of the Homeric epics as the credibility of incidents, characterization and even grammar. His name became proverbial for carping criticism.

p. 67, *Clymene*: It is unclear precisely to whom Pushkin was referring in this passage; scholars have yet to identify either this woman or her husband. Clymene ("Kliména" in Russian) is the name of several obscure nymphs and other female figures in Greek mythology, known chiefly as the mothers or wives of more famous characters, and Pushkin may have used the name simply as a pastoral pseudonym to conceal the identity of a married woman he loved. There are, however, some other tantalizing possibilities.

Virgil (whose work Pushkin knew) mentions (*Georgics* IV, 345) a sea-nymph Clymene attending a submarine working party of fellow nymphs and entertaining them with the Homeric tale of Hephaestus' wife Aphrodite's love affair with Ares, which interestingly Pushkin himself quotes in Canto IV, ll. 293–98 (see note to p. 109 on that passage). Could it be that Pushkin chose the pseudonym "Kliména" for a girl with whom he had read or discussed that tale at some literary soirée or other social event in St Petersburg?

A nymph of this name ("Clymène" in French) was the subject of a short pastoral comedy by Jean de La Fontaine (1621–95), a writer well known to Pushkin, and famous for his compilation of fables; this Clymène, who has been disillusioned by a first love, is portrayed as resisting the amorous advances of her present lover, offering him friendship only, though finally she gives in. In addressing these lines to a woman he admired who was disillusioned with her marriage partner, Pushkin may have had this Clymène in mind – he linked the names of Clymène and La Fontaine in a short French-language lyric he wrote in 1818 or 1819, during the period he was working on *Ruslan and Lyudmila*.

Pushkin used the name Kliména on one other occasion, six years before the publication of *Ruslan and Lyudmila*, when he was still a schoolboy of fifteen: under this pseudonym he addressed a short, light-hearted verse (entitled *To a lovely woman who took snuff*) to a woman he admired, generally believed to be a classmate's older sister, Yeléna Miháylovna Kantakuzina (*née* Gorchakóva) (1794–1854), already married to Geórgy Matvéyevich Kantakuzin (died 1857), who visited her brother at Pushkin's school in April 1814 – but there is no evidence that Kantakuzina, though remaining an acquaintance, was the woman referred to here. It is interesting that one of the classical Clymenes was, according to Homer (*Iliad* III, 144) and Ovid (*Heroides* XVII, 267), an attendant or confidante of Helen of Troy ("Yeléna" in Russian); so was the Kliména of the schoolboy verse perhaps not Yeléna Kantakuzina herself, but a friend or maid of hers who accompanied her on her visit to the school? However, the distance in time makes it unlikely that this Kliména is the one addressed in Canto 3.

p. 67, *you will shortly find yourself a laughing stock – and serve you right*: These two lines are a paraphrase of Pushkin's veiled threat, which reads literally: "and for your disgraced head there is now ready an avenging headdress" – a reference to the horns traditionally said to be sprouted by the dishonoured husbands of unfaithful wives (cf *Eugene Onegin* I, 12).

p. 77, *Bayán*: See fourth note to p. 9.

p. 81, *'The biggest head, the smallest brain!'* / *'I'll ride and ride and not ask leave,* / *and if I strike you I'll not grieve'*: Ruslán here quotes two Russian proverbs.

p. 89, *I took a pine tree on one shoulder*: Giants in fairy tales often carried uprooted pine trees as staves or weapons.

p. 90, *О витязь… судьбою*: This line supplied from the 1820 edition is missing from the 1828 text, presumably in error, since otherwise there would be no rhyme for line 458.

p. 92, *Их замыслы… молодым*: Pushkin shortened the 1820 text by six lines here – see Appendix, item H.

p. 93, *Each day… lead a quiet life (lines 1–16)*: After some straight-forwardly ironic lines (1–8), there follows a passage (lines 9–16) with several layers of significance.

At a layer just below the surface, Pushkin is referring to the fact, well-known to his friends, that during his years of youthful womanizing in St Petersburg (1817–20) he was obliged to spend several periods resting and convalescing from the pathological consequences of his lifestyle; it was indeed during these periods of convalescence that he wrote much of *Ruslan and Lyudmila*. Needless to say, once recovered, he soon returned to his old ways.

On another level commentators have seen a political reference here: on this interpretation the smile, blue eyes and charming voice (lines 11, 12) are those of the Emperor Alexander I, who was known for his smooth, cherubic appearance and (on the surface) great personal charm. Pushkin was already disillusioned with the Emperor by the time (1819) that he wrote these lines; indeed, the pages of his workbook in which he drafted them contain a doodled caricature of Alexander in the form of a siren (in classical mythology sirens were predatory creatures with a woman's face and a bird's plumage, who lured passing sailors to their death by the deceptive beauty of their singing).

A further – unconscious – irony of this passage is that it was through failing to take his own advice to "lie low and lead a quiet life" that a year later Pushkin so enraged Alexander by the indiscretion of some of his verses that the Emperor banished him from St Petersburg.

p. 93, *Zhukóvsky*: Vasíly Andréyevich Zhukóvsky (1783–1852) (not named by Pushkin in the text, though readers would have known immediately who was meant) was a respected poet and man of letters, and a friend of Pushkin's. Zhukóvsky had written, in around 1810, a narrative poem *The Twelve Sleeping Maidens*, which Pushkin here proceeds to summarize (lines 28–51), then good-humouredly to parody (lines 52 ff).

Sixteen years Pushkin's senior, Zhukóvsky first met the poet as a schoolboy; he immediately recognized the youngster's abilities and took him under his wing. He remained a firm friend and mentor to Pushkin throughout his life. Close to the imperial family (he was appointed tutor to the court in 1817), Zhukóvsky several times interceded with them on Pushkin's behalf. On Pushkin's death in 1837, at his widow's request, he became Pushkin's literary executor.

Zhukóvsky wrote a number of narrative poems, ballads and shorter lyric verses of his own, and in addition translated many works of European literature into Russian. One of Zhukóvsky's longer poems was a so-called "olden tale in two ballads", *The Twelve Sleeping Maidens*. It is a fanciful story of the supernatural, set (like *Ruslan and Lyudmila*) in a vaguely medieval Russia (hence "troubadour of mystic visions, of love, dreams, demons..." – lines 18, 19).

The first of the two "ballads" tells of an unhappy man minded to end the misery of his life one night by jumping off a cliff into the River Dnieper. At the last minute he is approached by the Devil and agrees to sell his soul for a ten-year life of power, riches and social success. He immediately uses his power to abduct twelve women, by whom he has twelve daughters within the year. But he loses interest in his "family", and they take refuge in a monastery, where the girls receive a godly upbringing. At the end of the ten years, frightened at the prospect of hell, he calls the girls back to pray for him. However, when the Devil comes at midnight to claim him, he negotiates a further bargain, in which he wins himself another ten years of life in return for the souls of the twelve daughters. Afterwards, though, life loses its joy for the old man: overcome by remorse and by pity for his daughters, he tries to make amends to God through alms-giving, church-building and religious observance. In his final illness his daughters, still unspoilt and innocent, join him in praying for God's forgiveness. In answer to their prayers St Nicholas arrives from heaven to intercede for them. When the Devil comes at midnight to claim his victims, God intervenes in anger. The girls are sent into a long sleep, from which they will only be awakened by the arrival of a pure-hearted man who has fallen in love with one of the girls without seeing her. The old man dies; his body is given a Christian burial nearby, but God allows the Devil to take his soul to hell for as long as the girls remain asleep. Supernaturally, castle walls arise around the house where the girls are sleeping, and the surrounding country is left desolate, choked by rocks and trees. Each month one of the girls awakes and roams the castle battlements, waiting and watching for the man who will deliver them. At the end of the month she returns to sleep and one of her half-sisters replaces her. Years pass.

The second ballad tells the story of a young and good-hearted warrior from Nóvgorod called Vadím. Vadím dreams of a veiled young woman beckoning him. He feels himself called to leave home and travel southwards. After some distracting adventures he is led to a desolate and rocky spot on the Dnieper. Exploring the vicinity, he finds a haunted tomb, a ruined church and then a castle on a wooded crag. On the castle walls he sees a girl, like the one in his dream, walking and watching. When the girl sees Vadím, she hurries down to meet him; the castle gates open; the other girls awake; and the first girl and Vadím are married in the magically restored church. The father's soul is now finally at peace. The eleven half-sisters spend the rest of their lives as nuns, visiting their father's tomb for prayer. When they die, their bodies are buried nearby, and their souls go to heaven.

Zhukóvsky's overlong tale is weak in its simplistic characterization, naive pietism and extravagantly fanciful plot; unlike *Ruslan and Lyudmila*, it is an entirely serious work, without Pushkin's irony and humour, but it is nonetheless narrated in musical verse of limpid, if somewhat archaic, charm. Pushkin, who genuinely liked and admired Zhukóvsky, teases him here in at least two ways: he succeeds in competently summarizing in twenty-four lines a story that Zhukóvsky takes 1,820 lines to tell, and he jokingly suggests that the twelve girls, instead of spending the time in their castle asleep, were actually wide awake, living it up and providing a rest and recreation facility for passing knights.

Zhukóvsky seems to have taken Pushkin's joke in good part. He was an enthusiastic admirer of *Ruslan and Lyudmila* and congratulated Pushkin warmly on its completion. Despite Zhukóvsky's generous reaction, Pushkin later regretted the parody; ten years afterwards he wrote: "For [the parody] I deserved a proper telling off, for showing a want of taste and sensitivity. It was unforgivable (especially at my age) to curry favour with the rabble by parodying a work of pure and poetic creativity." (*Refutation of Criticisms*, 1830)

p. 93, *Orpheus*: In Greek mythology Orpheus was a legendary poet and musician, who could move even beasts and inanimate objects with the beauty of his singing.

p. 94, *Но... ли я*: This line replaces six in the 1820 edition – see Appendix, item I.

p. 101, *Homer*: Homer (early first millennium BC), Greek poet, first figure in European literature, credited with the composition of the *Iliad* and *Odyssey*, lengthy epic poems about the Trojan war and its aftermath. Homer was famous for his descriptions of feasting (cf *Eugene Onegin* V, 36).

p. 101, *Parny*: Evarist-Désiré de Parny (1753–1814), a French poet famed for his intimate love lyrics.

p. 103, *Diana*: Diana [Artemis or Selene], in classical mythology goddess of hunting and the moon, was usually regarded as a virgin. Yet she gave herself in love to a handsome shepherd Endymion, whom she found asleep on a mountainside and whom she then sent into an eternal sleep so that she could visit him nightly without anyone's knowledge.

p. 105, *rusalkas*: See under note on the Prologue.

p. 109, *Just so did the lame blacksmith-god… how they laughed! (lines 293-8)*: Pushkin is referring to an entertaining tale about the Greek gods related by Homer (*Odyssey* VIII, 266–367). The lame blacksmith-god Hephaestus [Vulcan] was married to the goddess of love, Aphrodite [Venus]. Having learnt that his wife was having an affair with Ares [Mars], Hephaestus spread an invisible net over her bed and caught the two lovers in it. He then summoned the other gods to witness the scene, to their great amusement. A literal translation of lines 293–98 would be: "The lame blacksmith of Lemnos [Greek island associated with Hephaestus], having received the matrimonial crown from the hands of attractive Cytherea [Aphrodite], spread nets for her charms, revealing Cypris' [Aphrodite's] tender caprices to the jeering gods."

p. 110, *Ласкает... звон*: Pushkin shortened the 1820 text by eleven lines here – see Appendix, item J.

p. 113, *Delphíra*: Delphíra is seemingly a pseudonym for a woman Pushkin had fallen out of love with. Her identity is uncertain, but it may well be Yelizavéta Schott-Schedel, a St Petersburg courtesan whom Pushkin was in love with early in 1818: dressed as a hussar officer, she paid him an affectionate visit while he was convalescing from an illness at that time, though afterwards she apparently dropped him. She is commemorated in his lyric *Vyzdorovlénie* [Recovery], written when he was better:

> *...In the dark moments of life-threatening illness did you, gentle girl, stand over me, charmingly awkward in a soldier's uniform? Yes, I did see you; my blurred eyes recognized your beauty beneath that military dress... and suddenly I felt your breath, your tears, your moist kiss on my fevered brow... and then you vanished, like a lovely phantom! Cruel friend! you're wearing me out with infatuation: come, love is killing me!... Let me again glimpse, below the fearsome headgear of a soldier, your heavenly eyes, the cloak, the army belt, your legs so fetching in those marching boots... Do not delay, come quickly, my lovely warrior...*

It seems she didn't come.

p. 125, *The monk*: Monastic chronicles are our main source for the history of Kievan Rus. Karamzín relied heavily on them in compiling the relevant volumes of his *History of the Russian State*, on which Pushkin drew for the background of *Ruslan and Lyudmila*. Pushkin is here, tongue in cheek, inviting us to believe that his tale is attested in one of the old monastic chronicles.

p. 125, *Lída*: In an early draft Pushkin named the girl "Natasha", possibly recalling the Natasha (a maid to one of the ladies-in-waiting at court) on whom he had a crush as a schoolboy at Tsárskoye Seló in 1816, perhaps having fun with her in the park there, and whom he addressed in verse at the time. Pushkin several times at this period addressed love poems to "Lída", a typical name in conventional pastoral love poetry, sometimes at least using the name as a pseudonym for actual women he admired. In the present case, even if Pushkin did originally have a boyish escapade in mind, he is primarily making fun of the artificiality of the pastoral tradition in literature and contrasting its coy and frivolous heroines with his own more earnest and deeply felt portrait of Lyudmíla.

p. 126, *Укор... лепетала*: Pushkin dropped four lines from the 1820 edition here – see Appendix, item K.

p. 143, *gentle friend*: We do not know whom Pushkin was addressing in these lines (1–33). It may well have been the "Dorída" mentioned in the Epilogue (see second note to p. 165).

p. 147, *Vladímir the Resplendent*: See second note to p. 9.

p. 149, *Múrom-way*: A town on the River Oká, on the far north-eastern frontier of Kievan Rus, Múrom was home of one of the greatest heroes of Russian folklore preserved in the traditional ballads or *bylíny*, Ilyá Muromets (Ilyá of Múrom), who carried out many feats of superhuman strength and valour. Farláf is here "dropping" the name Múrom to suggest that his own fictitious exploit is on a par with those ascribed to the renowned Ilyá.

p. 149, *wood sprite*: See under note on the Prologue.

p. 151, *Pechenegs*: During the time of the historical Grand Prince Vladímir – and for a little before and afterwards, until they were replaced by the Polovtsy – Kiev's main neighbours to the south and south-east were the Pechenegs, a Turkic-speaking pagan tribe of tent-dwelling nomads. During the late tenth and early eleventh centuries there was frequent war between Kiev and the Pechenegs, with the Pechenegs besieging Kiev at least once during Vladímir's time, but on the whole the Kievans were successful in keeping the Pechenegs at bay.

p. 163, *A tale... of other years!*: See first note to p. 9.

p. 165, *Epilogue*: Pushkin's Epilogue to *Ruslan and Lyudmila* is an autobiographical document with only the most tenuous link to the rest of the work. It was not written till several months after completion of the main poem, too late for inclusion in the 1820 edition. For its background in the events of Pushkin's life, see page 198 of the Extra Material.

p. 165, *a fickle girlfriend*: Pushkin refers specifically to "Dorída", a pastoral pseudonym for a recent girlfriend who has now deserted him (perhaps also recalled in the last two lines of the Epilogue). Two short love lyrics addressed to Dorída survive from the year before Pushkin's banishment (May 1820), when he was completing work on *Ruslan and Lyudmila*. From the first we learn that she had golden hair, blue eyes and a pale complexion. In the second, written in the early months of 1820, Pushkin again extols Dorída's charms and declares himself convinced of the sincerity of her love for him. This Dorída may well also be the unnamed girl Pushkin addresses so fondly at the opening of Canto VI. The warmth of the affection evident in these last three passages, the lyrics and in Canto VI would account for the bitterness and disappointment Pushkin clearly felt at Dorída's subsequent betrayal.

p. 165, *Nevá's*: The Nevá is the river on whose estuary St Petersburg stands.

p. 167, *she whom I hymned in veneration / is lost to me for evermore*: Literally "gone from me for ever is the goddess of hushed hymns". Pushkin is "fading out" the last despairing lines of his Epilogue on a deliberately ambiguous note. Is his "goddess" the Dorída referred to above, the lost girlfriend he so recently worshipped (see second note to p. 165 above)? Or is she his Muse, goddess of poetic inspiration, who (he chooses to imagine) has also now deserted him? Or both?...

Extra Material

on

Alexander Pushkin's

Ruslan and Lyudmila

Alexander Pushkin's Life

Alexander Sergéyevich Púshkin was born in Moscow in 1799. *Family, Birth and*
He came of an ancient, but largely undistinguished, aristocratic *Childhood*
line. Some members of his father's family took a part in the
events of the reign of Tsar Borís Godunóv (1598–1605) and
appear in Pushkin's historical drama about that Tsar. Perhaps
his most famous ancestor – and the one of whom Pushkin was
most proud – was his mother's grandfather, Abrám Petróvich
Gannibál (or Annibál) (c.1693–1781), who was an African,
most probably from Ethiopia or Cameroon. According to
family tradition he was abducted from home at the age of
seven by slave traders and taken to Istanbul. There in 1704
he was purchased by order of the Russian foreign minister
and sent to Moscow, where the minister made a gift of him
to Tsar Peter the Great. Peter took a liking to the boy and
in 1707 stood godfather to him at his christening (hence his
patronymic Petróvich, "son of Peter"). Later he adopted the
surname "Gannibál", a Russian transliteration of Hannibal,
the famous African general of Roman times. Peter sent him
abroad as a young man to study fortification and military
mining. After seven years in France he was recalled to Russia,
where he followed a career as a military engineer. Peter's
daughter, the Empress Elizabeth, made him a general, and he
eventually died in retirement well into his eighties on one of
the estates granted him by the crown.

Pushkin had an older sister, Olga, and a younger brother,
Lev. His parents did not show him much affection as a child,
and he was left to the care of his grandmother and servants,
including a nurse of whom he became very fond. As was usual
in those days, his early schooling was received at home, mostly
from French tutors and in the French language.

School   In 1811 at the age of twelve Pushkin was sent by his parents to St Petersburg to be educated at the new Lyceum (Lycée, or high school) that the Emperor Alexander I had just established in a wing of his summer palace at Tsárskoye Seló to prepare the sons of noblemen for careers in the government service. Pushkin spent six happy years there, studying (his curriculum included Russian, French, Latin, German, state economy and finance, scripture, logic, moral philosophy, law, history, geography, statistics and mathematics), socializing with teachers and fellow students, and relaxing in the palace park. To the end of his life he remained deeply attached to his memories and friends from those years. In 1817 he graduated with the rank of collegial secretary, the tenth rank in the civil service, and was attached to the Ministry of Foreign Affairs, with duties that he was allowed to interpret as minimal. While still at the Lyceum Pushkin had already started writing poetry, some of which had attracted the admiration of leading Russian literary figures of the time.

St Petersburg 1817–20   Pushkin spent the next three years in St Petersburg living a life of pleasure and dissipation. He loved the company of friends, drinking parties, cards, the theatre and particularly women. He took an interest in radical politics. And he continued to write poetry – mostly lyric verses and epigrams on personal, amatory or political subjects – often light and ribald, but always crisply, lucidly and euphoniously expressed. Some of these verses, even unpublished, gained wide currency in St Petersburg and attracted the unfavourable notice of the Emperor Alexander I.

Pushkin's major work of this period was *Ruslan and Lyudmila*, a mock epic in six cantos, completed in 1820 and enthusiastically received by the public. Before it could be published, however, the Emperor finally lost patience with the subversiveness of some of Pushkin's shorter verses and determined to remove him from the capital. He first considered exiling Pushkin to Siberia or the White Sea, but at the intercession of high-placed friends of Pushkin's the proposed sentence was commuted to a posting to the south of Russia. Even so, some supposed friends hurt and infuriated Pushkin by spreading exaggerated rumours about his disgrace.

Travels in the South   Pushkin was detailed to report to Lieutenant-General Iván Inzov (1768-1845), who was at the time Commissioner for the Protection for Foreign Colonists in Southern Russia based at

Yekaterinosláv (now Dnepropetróvsk) on the lower Dnieper. Inzov gave him a friendly welcome, but little work to do, and before long Pushkin caught a fever from bathing in the river and was confined to bed in his poor lodgings. He was rescued by General Nikoláy Rayévsky, a soldier who had distinguished himself in the war of 1812 against Napoleon. Rayévsky, who from 1817 to 1824 commanded the Fourth Infantry Corps in Kiev, was travelling through Yekaterinosláv with his younger son (also called Nikoláy), his two youngest daughters María and Sófya, a personal physician and other attendants; they were on their way to join the elder son Alexander, who was taking a cure at the mineral springs in the Caucasus. General Rayévsky generously invited Pushkin to join them, and Inzov gave his leave.

The party arrived in Pyatigórsk, in the northern foothills of the Caucasus, in June. Pushkin, along with his hosts, benefited from the waters and was soon well again. He accompanied the Rayévskys on long trips into the surrounding country, where he enjoyed the mountain scenery and observed the way of life of the local Circassian and Chechen tribes. In early August they set off westwards to join the rest of the Rayévsky family (the General's wife and two older daughters) in the Crimea. On the way they passed through the Cossack-patrolled lands on the northern bank of the Kubán river and learnt more about the warlike Circassians of the mountains to the south.

General Rayévsky and his party including Pushkin met up with the rest of the family at Gurzúf on the Crimean coast, where they had the use of a villa near the shore. Pushkin enjoyed his time in the Crimea, particularly the majestic coastal scenery, the southern climate, and the new experience of living in the midst of a harmonious, hospitable and intelligent family. Before leaving the Crimea Pushkin travelled with the Rayévskys through the coastal mountains and inland to Bahchisaráy, an oriental town which had till forty years before been the capital of the Tatar khans of the Crimea and where the khans' palace still stood (and stands).

After a month in the Crimea it was time for the party to return to the mainland. During the summer General Inzov had been transferred from Yekaterinosláv to be governor of Bessarabia (the northern slice of Moldavia, which Russia had annexed from Turkey only eight years previously). His new headquarters was in Kishinyóv (*Chişinău*), the chief town of

Bessarabia. So it was to Kishinyóv that Pushkin went back to duty in September 1820. Pushkin remained there (with spells of local leave) till 1823.

Bessarabia 1820–23   Kishinyóv was still, apart from recently arrived Russian officials and soldiers, a raw near-eastern town, with few buildings of stone or brick, populated by Moldavians and other Balkan nationalities. Despite the contrast with St Petersburg, Pushkin still passed a lot of his time in a similar life-style of camaraderie, drinking, gambling, womanizing and quarrelling, with little official work. But he wrote too. And he also, as in the Caucasus and Crimea, took a close interest in the indigenous cultures, visiting local fairs and living for a few days with a band of Moldavian gypsies, an experience on which he later drew in his narrative poem *Gypsies*.

In the winter of 1820-21 Pushkin finished the first of his "southern" narrative poems, *A Prisoner in the Caucasus*, which he had already begun in the Crimea. (The epilogue he added in May 1821.) This poem reflects the experiences of his Caucasus visit. The work was published in August 1822. It had considerable public success, not so much for the plot and characterization, which were criticized even by Pushkin himself, but rather, as Pushkin realized, for its "truthful, though only lightly sketched, descriptions of the Caucasus and the customs of its mountain peoples".

Having completed *A Prisoner in the Caucasus*, Pushkin went on to write a narrative poem reflecting his impressions of the Crimea, *The Fountain of Bahchisaráy*. This was started in 1821, finished in 1823 and published in March 1824. It was also a great popular success, though again Pushkin dismissed it as "rubbish". Both poems, as Pushkin acknowledged, show the influence of Lord Byron, a poet whom, particularly at this period, Pushkin admired.

Just before his departure from Kishinyóv in 1823, Pushkin composed the first few stanzas of Chapter One of his greatest work, the novel-in-verse *Eugene Onegin*. It took him eight years to complete. Each chapter was published separately (except Chapters Four and Five, which came out together) between the years 1825 and 1832; the work was first published as a whole in 1833.

Odessa 1823–24   In the summer of 1823, through the influence of his friends in St Petersburg, Pushkin was posted to work for Count Miháil Vorontsóv, who had just been appointed Governor

General of the newly-Russianized region south of the Ukraine. Vorontsóv's headquarters were to be in Odessa, the port city on the Black Sea founded by Catherine the Great thirty years previously. Despite its newness Odessa was a far more lively, cosmopolitan and cultured place than Kishinyóv, and Pushkin was pleased with the change. But he only remained there a year.

Pushkin did not get on well with his new chief, partly because of temperamental differences, partly because Pushkin objected to the work Count Vorontsóv expected him to do, and partly because Pushkin had an affair with the Countess. Vorontsóv tried hard to get Pushkin transferred elsewhere, and Pushkin for his part became so unhappy with his position on the Count's staff that he tried to resign and even contemplated escaping overseas. But before matters came to a head the police intercepted a letter from Pushkin to a friend in which he spoke approvingly of the atheistic views of an Englishman he had met in the city. The authorities in St Petersburg now finally lost patience with Pushkin: he was dismissed from the service and sent to indefinite banishment on his mother's country estate of Miháylovskoye in the west of Russia. He left Odessa for Miháylovskoye in the summer of 1824; he had by now written two and a half chapters of *Eugene Onegin*, and had begun *Gypsies*.

Pushkin spent more than two years under police surveil- *Exile at Miháylovskoye* lance at Miháylovskoye. The enforced leisure gave him a lot of time for writing. Within a couple of months he had completed *Gypsies*, which was first published in full in 1827. *Gypsies* is a terser, starker, more thoughtful, and more dramatic work than *A Prisoner in the Caucasus* or *The Fountain of Bahchisaráy*; along with *Eugene Onegin* it marks a transition from the discursive romanticism of Pushkin's earliest years to the compressed realism of his mature style. At Miháylovskoye Pushkin progressively completed chapters III-VI of *Eugene Onegin*, many passages of which reflect Pushkin's observation of country life and love of the countryside. He also wrote his historical drama *Boris Godunov* at this period and his entertaining verse tale *Count Núlin*.

In November 1825 Alexander I died. He left no children, *The Decembrist Revolt* and there was initially confusion over the succession. In *1825* December some liberally-minded members of the army and the intelligentsia (subsequently known as the "Decembrists") seized the opportunity to attempt a coup d'état. This was put down by the new Emperor Nicholas I, a younger brother of Alexander's. Among the conspirators were several old friends of Pushkin, and he might well have joined them had he been at liberty. As it was, the leading conspirators were executed, and many of the rest were sent to Siberia for long spells of hard labour and exile. Pushkin feared that he too might be punished.

Rehabilitation 1826–31   The following autumn Pushkin was summoned unexpectedly to Moscow to see the new Emperor. Nicholas surprised Pushkin by offering him his freedom, and Pushkin assured Nicholas of his future good conduct. Pushkin complained that he had difficulty in making money from his writing because of the censorship, and Nicholas undertook to oversee Pushkin's work personally. In practice, however, the Emperor delegated the task to the Chief of the Secret Police, and, despite occasional interventions from Nicholas, Pushkin continued to have difficulty with the censors.

After a few months in Moscow Pushkin returned to St Petersburg, where he spent most of his time in the coming years, though he continued periodically to visit Moscow, call at the family's estates, and stay with friends in the country. In 1829 he made his only visit abroad, following the Russian army on a campaign into north-eastern Turkey. During the late 1820s he made several attempts to find a wife, with a view to settling down. In 1829 he met Natálya Gonchárova, whom he married early in 1831.

It was during the four years between his return from exile and his marriage that he wrote Chapter Seven (1827–28) and most of Chapter Eight (1829–31) of *Eugene Onegin*. In 1828 he also wrote *Poltáva* (published in 1829), a kind of historical novella-in-verse. This seems to have been the first attempt in Russian at a work of this kind based on the study of historical material. In its application of the imagination to real historical events, it prefigured Pushkin's later historical novel in prose *The Captain's Daughter* and helped to set a pattern for subsequent historical novels in Russia. It is also notable for the terse realism of its descriptions and for the pace and drama of its narratives and dialogues.

In the autumn of 1830 a cholera epidemic caused Pushkin to be marooned for a couple of months on another family estate, Boldíno, some 600 kilometres east of Moscow. He took advantage of the enforced leisure to write. This was when he virtually completed Chapter Eight of *Onegin*. He also composed at this time his collection of short stories in prose *The Tales of Bélkin*, another verse tale, *The Little House in Kolómna*, and his set of four one-act dramas known together as *The Little Tragedies*.

The 1830s were not on the whole happy years for Pushkin. *The Final Years 1831–37* His marriage, it is true, was more successful than might have been expected. Natálya was thirteen years his junior; her remarkable beauty and susceptibility to admiration constantly exposed her to the attentions of other men; she showed more liking for society and its entertainments than for intellectual or artistic pursuits or for household management; her fashionable tastes and social aspirations incurred outlays that the pair could ill afford; and she took little interest in her husband's writing. Nonetheless, despite all this they seem to have remained a loyal and loving couple; Natálya bore him four children in their less than six years of marriage, and she showed real anguish at his untimely death.

But there were other difficulties. Pushkin, though short of money himself and with a costly family of his own to maintain, was often called upon to help out his parents, his brother and sister and his in-laws and so fell ever deeper into debt. Both his wife and the Emperor demanded his presence in the capital so that he would be available to attend social and court functions, while he would much have preferred to be in the country, writing. Though Nicholas gave him intermittent support socially and financially, many at court and in the government, wounded by his jibes or shocked by his supposed political and sexual liberalism, disliked or despised him. And a new generation of writers and readers were beginning to look on him as a man of the past.

In 1831 Pushkin at length completed *Eugene Onegin*. The final Chapter Eight was published at the beginning of 1832, the first complete edition of the work coming out in 1833. But overall in these years Pushkin wrote less, and when he did write he turned increasingly to prose. In 1833 he spent another productive autumn at the Boldíno estate, producing his most famous prose novella, *The Queen of Spades*, and one of his finest narrative poems, *The Bronze Horseman*. He also developed in these years his interest in history, already evident in *Boris Godunov* and *Poltáva*: Nicholas I commissioned him to write a history of Peter the Great, but alas he only left copious notes for this at his death. He did, however, complete in 1833 a history of the eighteenth-century peasant uprising known as the Pugachóv rebellion, and he built on his research into this episode to write his longest work of prose fiction, *The Captain's Daughter* (1836). Over these years too he produced his five metrical fairy stories; these are mostly based on Russian folk tales, but one, *The Golden Cockerel* (1834), is an adaptation of one of Washington Irving's *Tales of the Alhambra*.

Writings   From his school days till his death Pushkin also composed well over 600 shorter verses, comprising many lyrics of love and friendship, brief narratives, protests, invectives, epigrams, epitaphs, dedications and others. He left numerous letters from his adult years that give us an invaluable insight into his thoughts and activities and those of his contemporaries. And, as a man of keen intelligence and interest in literature, he produced throughout his career many articles and shorter notes – some published in his lifetime, others not – containing a wide variety of literary criticism and comment.

It is indeed hard to name a literary genre that Pushkin did not use in his lifetime, or it would be truer to say that he wrote across the genres, ignoring traditional categories with his characteristic independence and originality. All his writing is marked by an extraordinary polish, succinctness and clarity; an extraordinary sense for the beauty of sounds and rhythms; an extraordinary human sympathy and insight; an extraordinary feel for what is appropriate to the occasion; and an extraordinary directness and naturalness of diction that is never pompous, insincere or carelessly obscure.

Death   Early in 1837 Pushkin's career was cut tragically short. Following a series of improper advances to his wife and insults to himself, he felt obliged to fight a duel with a young Frenchman who was serving as an officer in the imperial horse guards in St Petersburg. Pushkin was fatally wounded in the stomach and died at his home in St Petersburg two days later. The authorities denied him a public funeral in the capital for fear of demonstrations, and he was buried privately at the Svyatýe Góry monastery near Miháylovskoye, where his memorial has remained a place of popular pilgrimage.

Ruslan and Lyudmila

Pushkin had begun *Ruslan and Lyudmila* before he left *Composition*
school in 1817. But it was during his three years of freedom
and pleasure in St Petersburg (see page 188) that he wrote the
bulk of the work, especially in the recuperative intervals that
his unhealthy lifestyle imposed on itself. When *Ruslan and
Lyudmila* was finished he was still under twenty-one years old.
It was his first major work. Pushkin read the completed poem
to his literary friends in March 1820.

Within a few weeks, before the work could be published,
Alexander I, having finally lost patience with the subversiveness
(as he saw it) of some of Pushkin's other verses, banished
Pushkin from the capital. Pushkin set off in early May. En
route to his final destination in Moldavia Pushkin made an
excursion to the Caucasus and the Crimea, and it was in the
Caucasus, in July 1820, that he wrote the epilogue to the
poem.

Through the efforts of the absent poet's friends *Ruslan* *Publication and*
and Lyudmila was published in St Petersburg around the end *Reception*
of July 1820. The epilogue, ready too late, was published
separately in September. The poem was an immediate
success with the public, but it set off a furious battle among
the critics, some of whom attacked it for absurdity, coarse
language, indecency or "deficiency of lofty sentiments". One
distinguished writer of an older generation, Iván Dmítriev
(1760–1837), commented: "I see here neither sense nor senti-
ment; I see only sensuality."

Some modern commentators such as Yúry Lotman suggest
that what upset the critics was not so much the liberty of
certain descriptive passages as Pushkin's subversiveness in
combining the traditionally distinct genres of narrative poetry
(e.g. epic, didactic, national-heroic, magic, humorous) in a
single work and in substituting irony for morality.

Much later, in 1828, Pushkin had *Ruslan and Lyudmila*
republished with the epilogue; he added the famous prologue,
and he made a few other revisions, including (though he
repudiated the charge of "indecency") the excision of a
couple of the more *risqué* passages. It is the 1828 text that is
normally regarded as the definitive version and is the basis of
this edition. The excisions from the 1820 edition are given in
the Appendix on pages 212 to 219.

Description *Ruslan and Lyudmila* is a narrative poem in six parts (or "cantos"). Together with the brief dedication and the prologue and epilogue, it comprises 2,822 lines of unstanzaed, irregularly rhymed iambic tetrameters – lines of eight or nine syllables with the stress normally falling on the even-numbered ones. It is Pushkin's longest poetical work apart from his verse-novel *Eugene Onegin*.

Literary Significance Even before Pushkin left school, his talent had brought him to the notice of leading figures in Russian literature. During the following three years Pushkin moved freely in St Petersburg literary circles. He associated especially with writers of the modernist group, led by the eminent poet Zhukóvsky. These writers wanted to drive Russian literature forwards by use of a modern and flexible Russian language, while steering it within the current of Western European writing, which they knew and admired. It had for some years been this group's ambition to produce a major Russian work in the modern style, but neither Zhukóvsky (who had contemplated a heroic poem on the subject of Grand Prince Vladímir of Kiev) nor any of the others had found the necessary time or inspiration. When Pushkin appeared in 1817 with his first ideas for an extended narrative poem on a legendary Russian subject, they encouraged him and followed his progress with attention and growing enthusiasm. *Ruslan and Lyudmila* became a demonstration piece for the new style, a challenge to the constrained tastes and conventions of earlier Russian literature. And three years later Pushkin's literary mentors were delighted with the outcome – so much so that Zhukóvsky presented his portrait to the twenty-year-old Pushkin with the generous inscription "To the victorious pupil from the vanquished teacher, on that day of high triumph when he finished his poem *Ruslan and Lyudmila*. Good Friday, 26 March 1820."

Origins There has been much argument over the origins of *Ruslan and Lyudmila*. Different scholars have attributed elements of the poem – its personalities, incidents, attitudes, style – to an extraordinary variety of sources, foreign and Russian, literary, historical and theatrical. It is indeed possible to glimpse in the poem reflections of Greco-Roman classics – Homer and others; of the works of Western European writers – Ariosto (*Orlando Furioso*), Torquato Tasso (*Gerusalemme Liberata*), Wieland (*Oberon*), La Fontaine (*Les amours de Psyché et Cupidon*), Antoine Hamilton (*Contes*), Voltaire (*La Pucelle d'Orléans*),

Parny (*Isnel et Aslega*), Macpherson (the Ossianic poems); and of the achievements of Russian culture – the Russian twelfth-century epic *Slovo o polku Igoreve*; Russian epic folk songs (*bylíny*, collections of which had recently been published); Russian folk tales (as collected by Chulkov, Levshin and others in the late eighteenth century); Russian heroic poems of the turn of the century by Karamzín (*Ilyá Muromets*), Kheraskov (*Bahariyana*) and others; poetry by Bogdanóvich (*Dúshenka*) and Zhukóvsky (ballads such as *The Twelve Sleeping Maidens*); Karamzín's *History of the Russian state* (the relevant volumes of which were published early in 1818); and contemporary fairy-tale ballets and operas (such as the popular *Rusálka of the Dnieper*).

Pushkin indisputably drew much of the story of *Ruslan* *Sources for the Plot* *and Lyudmila* from Russian folklore. The opening scene is reminiscent of descriptions of lengthy banquets given in Kiev by "Prince Vladímir-the-Sun" in numerous Russian *bylíny* (folk songs). One, for example, begins with lines about Vladímir presiding at a feast attended by "princes, nobles, valiant warriors and wealthy guests", where all are eating and drinking and having a good time, except one disaffected noble, who refuses to drink or eat. Another begins with a similar feast and goes on to tell of three warriors who answer Vladímir's appeal to set out on a distant mission. Another tells of a feast given by Vladímir for his daughter's wedding, during which minstrels play the gusli. Some *bylíny* mention sieges of Kiev or other Russian cities by eastern hordes; one mentions a magic creature's palace and garden.

Russian folk tales also provided Pushkin with material. One tells of a tsar whose wife is carried off by the wizard Kashchéy to his enchanted palace on an inaccessible mountain top and who then sends his three sons out to rescue her. Another folk tale relates how the hero Yeruslan Lazarevich (note the similar name to Pushkin's hero) encounters a warrior's severed head on a battlefield of corpses and wins a special sword. A story about the folk hero Ilyá of Múrom tells of how he awakened a beautiful girl from an enchanted sleep into which she had been put by a cunning magician named Chernomór. Other story-writers of the eighteenth century, drawing on Russian folk themes, had told of heroines seized by evil wizards, accommodated in luxurious chambers, mocking or defying their captors, succumbing to an enchanted sleep, and rescued by daring heroes and friendly sorcerers.

One version of the story of the Firebird tells of a tsar with a magic garden. He sends out his three sons on a distant mission, and after an initial journey they come to a place where the road divides into three. The hero among the sons takes a road that eventually leads to a palace where he abducts a beautiful princess. On the way home the hero-prince and the princess lie down to sleep; his jealous brothers find them; they kill the hero-prince, cut his body in pieces, seize the princess and carry her home. Meanwhile a bird who has found the murdered prince flies to a distant land to fetch water from two wells, from one the water of death and from the other the water of life. When the two kinds of water are sprinkled on the prince's dismembered body the pieces come together and he lives again. On his return home the couple are reunited, the tsar holds a grand wedding feast in their honour, and the wicked brothers for punishment are given menial jobs in the royal household.

In another folk tale a prince about to marry has his bride snatched from him by a wizard (in this case Kashchéy) and rides off on a long expedition to rescue her. In another there is a malign wood-sprite in the form of a dwarf with extremely long whiskers. In another the hero on his wanderings comes across a battlefield strewn with dead soldiers and broken weapons. In another tale a princess turns herself into a snake by stamping her foot on the ground.

These and other elements are cleverly woven together by Pushkin to form an entirely new story with characters whose personalities and interactions are far subtler and more interesting, as well as funnier, than those of the stereotypes of the old folk tales and folk songs.

A Demonstration Piece Pushkin was certainly aware of all this material, Russian and Western European. Even as a schoolboy he was remarkably well read both in Russian and in French (through which he knew not only French works, but many of the classics of European literature in translation); Latin and German too figured in his curriculum. So it is not surprising that, as a lively and resourceful youngster, already confident of his poetical abilities, he should have wanted show off his literary education by reflecting as much of it as he could in this tour-de-force of a demonstration piece. So he set out to show – and successfully showed – that a concoction of motifs from traditional Russian legends, from Greco-Roman classics and from Western

European epic, chivalric, romantic and satiric sources could be served up attractively in a modern Russian idiom, spiced with parody, humour and contemporary observation, and garnished with fluent and polished verse.

One might expect a demonstration piece like this to result *Style* in a tediously precious and over-erudite display of literary virtuosity, burdensome and even distasteful to the reader. Nothing could be more wrong. It is a sure mark of Pushkin's genius that, virtuoso though he is, he hides his virtuosity within a work that is exceptionally easy, enjoyable and entertaining to read. *Ruslan and Lyudmila* is a good story, fast moving, packed with inventive episodes, skilfully recounted in beautiful language and brilliant verse; there are vivid narratives blending realism and fantasy; there are erotic episodes and gory battle scenes; there are lyrical descriptions of landscapes; there is much comedy and a little pathos; and the whole is suffused with wry observation and good humour. It is a poem of constant shifts of mood and style, like shot silk showing different textures, lights and patterns as it moves, but held together by Pushkin's identity as narrator, commentator and digresser; now involved with his story, now detached; now serious, now joking; now lyrical, now ironic – a technique that he was later to use again in his greatest work, *Eugene Onegin*. The originality of *Ruslan and Lyudmila* is not (as we have seen) in the elements of the story; it is in the skilfulness of their combination and in the engaging humour and informality with which they are presented.

Although set in a legendary past of daring knights and dis- *Characterization* tressed damsels, of magicians and monstrosities, the appeal of *Ruslan and Lyudmila* lies also, paradoxically, in its modernity. From the moment when, only thirty lines in, Ruslán, dying to get into bed with Lyudmíla, starts to fiddle with his moustache in impatience at the celebrated bard's obligatory encomium, we realize that this is not to be a work of reverential medievalism. An important element in Pushkin's originality and genius is shown in the liveliness and individuality of the characterization: Pushkin has deliberately peopled his fanciful world with a variety of characters that are not the traditional stereotypes of folklore or medieval romance, but display emotions, mannerisms and interactions drawn, with a tinge of satire, from contemporary life. Ruslán is the young guards officer, socially diffident still and inarticulate, instinctive more than intellectual, fierce fighter when aroused, but good-hearted, steady and considerate.

Lyudmíla is the lively but shy seventeen-year-old, fresh to society from a sheltered upbringing, "a little scatterbrained" but mettlesome, girlishly self-dramatizing but sincere and loyal in her affections. Naína is the envenomed old spinster; blunt, brusque and imperious. Chernomór is the corrupt old St Petersburg grandee, believing himself above the law; pompous, devious and warped; preying on others to gratify his pleasures; indulging himself in a fabulous palace with fabulous servants and fabulous gardens amid surroundings of icy desolation. And so on with Rogdáy, Farláf and young Ratmír (closest to Pushkin himself), Vladímir, and the Head. Even the venerable Finn is less the pagan *shaman* than a thinly disguised Orthodox holy man, who has exchanged a turbulent past for solitude, study and contemplation – prototype of the old chronicler-monk in *Boris Godunov*. It is the observed reality of the characters, as much as the inventive unreality of the story, that holds our interest.

Pushkin's Later Work   Pushkin never produced another work like *Ruslan and Lyudmila*. More than ten years later he brought out several much shorter folk tales in his inimitably fluent and melodious verse (though in different metres). But they are essentially a straight retelling of old tales in the traditional way – without authorial comment, digression, overt irony or overlay of contemporary diction or characterization. The next narrative poems that Pushkin wrote after *Ruslan and Lyudmila* in the first years of his banishment – *A Prisoner in the Caucasus, The Fountain of Bahchisaráy* and *Gypsies* – are completely different in subject matter, tone and style, lacking the variety, the lightness and the humour.

As mentioned above, the one later work of Pushkin's to bear comparison with *Ruslan and Lyudmila* is his verse-novel *Eugene Onegin*. Although *Eugene Onegin* is a story of modern characters in an entirely modern setting, the two works share a number of characteristics. The two are Pushkin's longest narrative poems by far; they both have simple underlying plots, but a wealth of incident; they both present similarly well observed and many-sided characters; they both contain evocative descriptions, interspersed with social and literary comment and authorial intervention; they are both written in the same lively and informal idiom; and they are both infused with similar irony and humour. Pushkin himself acknowledges the link in the second stanza of *Eugene Onegin*:

Fans of my *Ruslan and Lyudmila*,
I'd like to have you meet
without preamble or ado
my novel's hero...

suggesting that the two works will appeal to the same public. As a Russian commentator has observed: "*Ruslan and Lyudmila* is to *Eugene Onegin* what youth is to adulthood" (V.A. Koshelev, *Pervaya Kniga Pushkina*, Tomsk 1997, page 216).

The poem that excited St Petersburg in 1820 – the original *Second Edition* six cantos framed by the Ossian quotation, and prefaced by the provocative dedication – was not only a hugely successful demonstration piece, an exquisite composition, an engaging story and an intriguing character study: it was also a youthful work of uncompromising optimism and cheerfulness – love triumphant, goodness vindicated and outrage and treachery not only vanquished but forgiven. The second edition, which Pushkin published eight years later, was a different work, in two ways.

First, Pushkin's demonstration piece had done its job: it had made its literary point; it had won the author a lasting reputation; by 1828 it was already literary history. The artist's canvas had been exhibited, discussed, admired, acclaimed; it was time now to put it in a frame and hang it up in the picture gallery for the enjoyment of posterity. That was the function of Pushkin's new prologue: to repackage *Ruslan and Lyudmila* for the future as just an entertaining fairy story, which is indeed how it has since been treated in the Russian-speaking world.

Secondly, Pushkin's own outlook on life had changed. He had of course matured from a youth of twenty to a man of twenty-eight. But more importantly, the cataclysm of April-May 1820 – his forced departure from St Petersburg and the events surrounding it – had shaken the young man's confidence in himself, in his society and in his future. The epilogue was a product of these events, and, although by 1828 they too were past history, and Pushkin had long regained much of his native nonchalance and gaiety, the boundless optimism and cheerfulness that had characterized *Ruslan and Lyudmila* at its first appearance had gone for ever. This was no doubt why in 1828 Pushkin decided to attach the epilogue permanently to the poem – as a wry comment on the overconfidence and overtrustfulness of youth, and on the boyish spontaneity, never to be recaptured, of his 1820 masterpiece.

Western Awareness   If *Ruslan and Lyudmila* is known as a title in the West, it is normally (as with so many of Pushkin's works) through opera. Shortly after Pushkin's death the Russian composer Glinka based an opera on Pushkin's poem; it had its first performance in St Petersburg in 1842. The overture has found a place in the repertoire of popular classical music outside Russia. The opera itself, however, is rarely performed in the West. Though Glinka's music is innovative and delightful, his librettists made drastic changes to Pushkin's story and used his lines for only about ten per cent of the text. The resultant libretto is dramatically and psychologically feeble. The opera deserves to be better known for its music, but Pushin's original poem deserves much greater recognition for its literary significance, its beauty and its fun.

Note on the Translation

Aims In translating *Ruslan and Lyudmila* into English my overriding aim has been faithfully to communicate the *meaning* of Pushkin's text to English readers. That, in my view, is the translator's first duty.

The translator's second duty – almost as important – is faithfully to convey the *spirit* of the original – to match its character, style and "tone of voice". So I have striven, too, to reproduce in clear, fluent and modern English Pushkin's clear, fluent and modern Russian. And as Pushkin has varied his "tone of voice" (as he constantly does) according to the effect he wants to produce – whether solemn, or serious, or polemical, or straightforward, or lyrical, or funny, or ironic – so I have tried to do the same.

I have made it my third task, as far as is compatible with the first two, to reproduce the *form* of the original. I have used the same metre as Pushkin, the iambic tetrameter. I have used the same number of lines as Pushkin, normally matching my lines with his, except where the natural structure of an English sentence leads me to do otherwise. This was not an objective I set myself at the start, but I have found that the number of syllables needed to produce an adequate English translation of Pushkin's sentences happens, *approximately and on average*, to match the number of syllables in Pushkin's Russian. So keeping, sentence by sentence, to Pushkin's lines has been a good discipline for me, and will be convenient to the student or bilingual reader.

Russian words carry a heavy stress, but the stressed syllable *Proper Names* is hard to predict, especially in proper names. Conventional English pronunciations (e.g. R<u>u</u>slan, Vl<u>a</u>dimir, N<u>e</u>va) often differ from the correct Russian ones (Rusl<u>a</u>n, Vlad<u>i</u>mir, Nev<u>a</u>). It is the Russian pronunciations that I have used in constructing the iambic rhythms of my translation, and to help the English-speaker read the lines as they are meant to sound, I have used an acute accent to indicate the stressed syllable on all Russian proper names (e.g. Ruslán, Vladímir, Nevá).

In one respect I have not attempted to imitate Pushkin's *Rhyme* original. Pushkin's lines are rhymed throughout, in an irregular pattern. But I am convinced that to try to recreate a similar rhyme scheme in English would be futile. My English rhymes could only ever be *different* from Pushkin's; they could never produce *the same* sound effect. Moreover, it is simply impossible in English, because of the nature of the language, to produce the same wealth and spontaneity of rhyme that any Russian poet can produce – and Pushkin is more than *any* Russian poet!

More importantly, I am also convinced that the attempt to produce a rhymed version of *Ruslan and Lyudmila* would be incompatible with the achievement of my first two aims. First, it is impossible to translate a lengthy poem like this into rhymed English lines without doing unacceptable violence to the natural meaning of the original words. Secondly, the strain of creating rhymed lines in English will force an unacceptable distortion of Pushkin's style and tone. Thirdly, a modern English readership's reaction to a rhymed narrative poem is very different from the reaction of Pushkin's Russian readership: it is hard for lengthy passages of rhymed verse in modern English not to seem either comical or stilted. In short, I am convinced that rhyme is an obstacle, not an aid, to the faithful translation of Pushkin's poetry into English.

I have therefore translated *Ruslan and Lyudmila* into blank verse. (The only exception is the last couplet of each canto, which I have rhymed in order to give a satisfying sense of closure, like a perfect cadence in music.) Of course, the English reader will miss the inimitable harmony of Pushkin's rhymes. But anyone who wants to enjoy that has no alternative but to learn Russian. The purpose of my translation is to bring to the English reader who, for any reason, *has not learnt* Russian the opportunity, too long withheld, of enjoying the many other delights of Pushkin's writing.

Alternatives to Rhyme   There are, however, ways of reproducing some of Pushkin's music in English that need not conflict with the overriding aims of faithfulness in meaning and spirit. I have tried to make up for the absence of rhyme by producing a translation that *sounds* attractive in other ways – notably through appropriate rhythms, repetitions, alliterations and assonances. In ways like this I hope I have produced a version that will give the English reader, through its sounds, a little of the same pleasure that the Russian reader receives from Pushkin's incomparable word music.

Acknowledgements

Translating and editing *Ruslan and Lyudmila* must, because of the nature of Pushkin's tale and the quality of his writing, be one of the most enjoyable tasks in literary translation. My especial thanks, therefore, are due to Alessandro Gallenzi, who has for a second time in a decade entrusted me with this task and caused this uniquely full edition of Pushkin's unrecognized masterpiece to be presented to the English-reading public.

Secondly, I want to thank my wife Elizabeth for providing me with the support and time I needed to revise the translation and extend the commentary.

I should also record once again my gratitude to Simon Blundell, Librarian of the Reform Club in London, for his help in the research I undertook for the first edition in 2005.

Ruslan and Lyudmila, overshadowed as it has been by Pushkin's later work, has seldom, even in Russia, received the serious attention it deserves. So there are few predecessors whom I can thank for assistance in elucidating the translation or in developing the commentary and other background material. I have of course drawn on the notes and commentaries in the various multi-volume editions of Pushkin's collected works published in Russia over the last seventy years, but their explanations of biographical, historical, mythological and literary references, though a useful starting point, are brief and far from exhaustive. Much the fullest and most informative account I have found of the background to the work – its literary antecedents, composition, publication and critical reception – is in V.A. Koshelev's excellent *Pervaya Kniga Pushkina* [*Pushkin's First Book*] of 1997. There is also much useful material in the first volume of B. Tomashevsky's great work on *Pushkin*, first published in the Soviet Union in 1956. Finally, I must also record my thanks to Professor L. Arinshtein of the Russian Cultural Foundation for answering questions I put to him about nameless or pseudonymous friends that Pushkin alludes to here and there in *Ruslan and Lyudmila*.

– Roger Clarke, 2009

Select Bibliography

Standard Editions:
The standard text of *Ruslan and Lyudmila* is available in numerous collections of Pushkin's works, published in the Soviet Union and in Russia during the last half-century and more, for example:

Sobranie Sochineniy Pushkina, volume III (Moscow: *Gosudarstvennoye Izdatelstvo Hudozhestvennoy Literatury*, 1959–62)

This ten-volume collection of Pushkin's works is also available on-line through the *Russkaya virtualnaya biblioteka* at www. rvb.ru/pushkin/toc.htm

Biographies:
There are many biographies of Pushkin; the most thorough recent work in English is:

Binyon, T.J., *Pushkin: A Biography* (London: HarperCollins, 2002)

Additional Recommended Background Material:
Koshelev, V.A., *Pervaya Kniga Pushkina* (Tomsk: *Izdatelstvo Vodoley*, 1997)
Lotman, Yury, *Statyi i issledovaniya: Pushkin* (St Petersburg, 1995)
Martin, Janet, *Medieval Russia, 980–1584* (Cambridge: Cambridge University Press, 1995)
Tomashevsky, B., *Pushkin* (Moscow-Leningrad: *Izdatelstvo Akademii Nauk*, 1956)

Appendix

The First Edition of 1820

The text of *Ruslan and Lyudmila* presented in this volume follows the 1828 edition, the second published by Pushkin during his lifetime and the one normally treated as definitive. In publishing the 1828 edition Pushkin introduced a number of changes from the first edition of 1820. He included the Epilogue and lines 147–153 of Canto VI, which, though written in 1820, had not been completed in time for printing; he added the famous Prologue (see note on page 168); he made some minor corrections, but he also cut several passages, sometimes with consequential adjustments to adjacent lines. The eleven passages cut from the 1820 edition, together with adjacent lines where these were altered, are set out in Russian and English below.

Why did Pushkin make these cuts? Although the first edition had been widely acclaimed by the public, it had stirred up considerable controversy in literary circles: as Pushkin himself afterwards observed in an unpublished article:[1]

It was criticized for indecency because of several faintly erotic descriptions; because of some lines that have been omitted from the second edition –

Oh dreadful sight! – the feeble wizard
caressing with his shrivelled hands… etc;

because of the introduction to I-don't-know-which of the cantos –

What good was it to hide my verses… etc;[2]

and because of the parody of *The Twelve Sleeping Maidens*…[3]

---

1. *Rebuttal of criticisms*, 1830.
2. The opening of Canto 3.
3. Canto 4, l. 28 ff, see second note to p. 93.

Pushkin resented these charges of 'indecency'. He felt that the passages concerned were milder than many found in admired authors of the past: for instance, the passage at the end of his Canto V beginning 'Oh dreadful sight!...' describing the impotent wizard's attempts to make love to the sleeping Lyudmíla, was a much toned down version of a similar description in canto V of Ariosto's *Orlando Furioso*. In the 1828 edition he made few concessions to the critics of 'indecency', dropping only two of the many passages to which prudish critics had objected (E and J below).

One can only speculate on Pushkin's motives for most of the cuts, several of which contain (as do E and J) lively and entertaining material. Some (e.g. A, B, C, F, I and K) may be because the mature writer considered some lines too weak or juvenile. Alternatively (in the case of A, B, D, F and G, for instance), he may have wanted simply to shorten episodes that seemed on reflection overlong. More obviously, Pushkin will have made cut H because its ironic references to the eccentric beliefs of members of Alexander I's circle were no longer topical under his successor in 1828.

Whatever Pushkin's precise motives, the cuts in this Appendix should give readers some added insight into Pushkin's mind and enable them to reconstruct his first major work in the form in which it broke upon the Russian literary world and laid the basis for his reputation.

*Стихи первого издания (1820), изъятые или переработанные
для второго издания (1828)*

А. Песнь первая, после стиха 363:

Руслан, не знаешь ты мученья
Любви, отверженной навек.
Увы! ты не сносил презренья.
И что же, странный человек!
И ты ж тоскою сердце губишь.
Счастливец! ты любим, как любишь.

К чему рассказывать, мой сын…   364

Б. Песнь первая, вместо стихов 402-406:

В надежде сладостных наград,   402
В восторге пылкого желанья,
Творю поспешно заклинанья,
Зову духов – и виноват! –
Безумный, дерзостный грабитель,
Достойный Черномора брат,
Я стал Наины похититель.
Лишь загадал, во тьме лесной
Стрела промчалась громовая,…   406

В. Песнь вторая, после стиха 20:

Ужели Бог нам дал одно
В подлунном мире наслажденье?
Вам остаются в утешенье
Война и Музы и вино.

Когда Рогдай неукротимый…   21

Lines of the first edition of 1820 that Pushkin excised or reworked for the edition of 1828

A. Canto I, after line 363:

"Ruslán, you've never felt the pain
of love repeatedly rejected –
it hurts! You've never known contempt.
So why, strange fellow that you are –
why blight your inner self with heartache?
You're lucky! You're in love, and loved.

"What good is it, my son, to try...   364

B. Canto I, in place of lines 402-406:

I hoped for pleasure as reward: 402
desire inflamed my senses, and
I hastily intoned my spells;
I summoned spirits. I was guilty –
a mindless, shameless woman-snatcher,
no better than a Chernomór:
Naína's rapist, that's what I was!
My spells once uttered, in the darkened
forest a thunderbolt crashed down,...   406

C. Canto II, after line 20:

Don't think that God has granted us
only one pleasure in this world.
There's plenty left to cheer you up –
like fighting, drinking, writing verse.

Rogdáy, though, was implacable...   21

Г. Песнь вторая, вместо стихов 215-216:

Людмила, где твоя светлица?   215
Где ложе радости младой?
Одна, с ужасной тишиной
Лежит несчастная девица…   216

Д. Песнь вторая, после стиха 230:

Вы знаете, что наша дева
Была одета в эту ночь,
По обстоятельствам, точь-в-точь
Как наша прабабушка Ева.
Наряд невинный и простой!
Наряд Амура и природы!
Как жаль, что вышел он из моды!
Пред изумленною княжной
Три девы красоты чудесной,
В одежде легкой и прелестной,
Явились, молча подошли
И поклонились до земли.   234

Е. Песнь вторая, после стиха 329:

Повсюду роз живые ветки   330
Цветут и дышат по тропам,
Усеянным песком алмазным;
Игривым и разнообразным
Волшебством дивный сад блестит.
Но безутешная Людмила…   332

Ж. Песнь вторая, после стиха 353:

О люди, странные созданья!
Меж тем как тяжкие страданья
Тревожат, убивают вас,
Обеда лишь наступит час –
И вмиг вам жалобно доносит

D. Canto II, in place of lines 215-216:

this wasn't the bright room she knew,   215
wasn't the bed a young bride wanted!
Alone, and frightened by the silence,
the poor girl lay in misery...   216

E. Canto II, after line 230:

You'll understand that our young lady
was wearing for that special night
(things being so) the very outfit
that our great-grandmamma Eve wore –
an outfit plain and unassuming,
as Love and Nature both prescribed.
A shame such dress is out of fashion!
Then there appeared without a sound,
to the princess's great surprise,
three wonderfully lovely girls,
dressed lightly, charmingly. They came
towards her and made low obeisance.   234

F. Canto II, after line 329:

Fresh sprays of fragrant roses flowered   330
everywhere alongside paths
spread with a gravel ground from diamonds.
The whole amazing garden gleamed
with magic, playful and diverse.
Lyudmíla, though, disconsolate...   332

G. Canto II, after line 353:

What oddities you people are!
Distress may drive you to distraction,
even to thoughts of suicide,
but once your dinnertime has come –
then straightaway your empty stomach

Пустой желудок о себе
И им заняться тайно просит.
Что скажем о такой судьбе?

Моя прекрасная Людмила…   354

З. Песнь четвертая, вместо стихов 6-9:

Женитьбы наши безопасны…   6
Мужьам, девицам молодым
Их замыслы не так ужасны.
Неправ фернейский злой крикун!
Всё к лучшему: теперь колдун
Иль магнетизмом лечит бедных
И девушек худых и бледных,
Пророчит, издает журнал –
Дела достойные похвал!
Но есть волшебники другие…   9

И. Песнь четвертая, вместо стихов 52-54:

И что ж, возможно ль?… нам солгали!   52
Дерзну ли истину вещать?
Дерзну ли ясно описать
Не монастырь уединенный,
Не робких инокинь собор,
Но… трепещу! в душе смущенный,
Дивлюсь – и потупляю взор.

Младой Ратмир, направя к югу…   54

Й. Песнь четвертая, вместо стихов 325-330:

О страшный вид! Волшебник хилый   325
Ласкает сморщенной рукой
Младые прелести Людмилы;
К ее пленительным устам
Прильнув увядшими устами,

starts sending grumpy messages
covertly claiming your attention.
There's no explaining human nature!

So my ineffable Lyudmíla...   354

H. Canto IV, in place of lines 6-9:

we can be wed in safety now...   6
their magic gives less cause for dread
to bridegrooms and young brides alike.
Voltaire was wrong, that noisy cynic!
Things *are* all for the best:* now wizards
use magnetism* to cure the frail
and girls who're skinny and anaemic,
they prophesy, they publish journals* –
commendable pursuits, each one!
There's wizardry of other sorts, though...   9

I. Canto IV, in place of line 52-54:

But – can it be so?... We've been lied to!   52
Dare I disclose the naked facts?
Dare I present a truthful picture
not of an isolated convent,
not of meek nuns at prayer in church,
but of... I'm shaking! Disconcerted
and shocked, I've turned my eyes away.

Ratmír, Lyudmíla's youngest suitor...   54

J. Canto IV, in place of lines 325-330:

Oh dreadful sight! – the feeble wizard   325
caressing with his shrivelled hands
Lyudmíla's young and lovely figure!
He's pressing his own withered lips
against those lovely lips of hers

Он, вопреки своим годам,
Уж мыслит хладными трудами
Сорвать сей нежный, тайный цвет,
Хранимый Лелем для другого;
Уже… но бремя поздних лет
Тягчит бесстыдника седого –
Стоная, дряхлый чародей
В бессильной дерзости своей
Пред сонной девой упадает;
В нем сердце ноет, плачет он,
Но вдруг раздался рога звон,
И кто-то карлу вызывает.   330

К. Песнь пятая, после стиха 287:

В руках Руслана чародей
Томился в муках ожиданья;
И князь не мог отвесть очей
От непонятного созданья…
Но головы в тот самый час…   288

and, in defiance of his years,
means now to bend his frigid efforts
to snatch this soft and shrinking bloom that
the Love-god's saving for another;
and now... The heavy load of years, though,
were weighing down the shameless greybeard.
For all his impotent bravado,
the senile sorcerer collapsed
beside the slumbering girl and groaned;
his heart was hurting, he was sobbing.
But then a sudden horn call sounded –
someone was challenging the dwarf!   330

K. Canto V, after line 287:

Still prisoner of Ruslán, the wizard
endured an agony of waiting;
the prince meanwhile could only stare
at the extraordinary creature...
In that same hour the Head's protracted...   288

Notes on Appendix

p. 217, *Voltaire... Things are all for the best*: Literally, "the cynical loud-mouth of Ferney..." Ferney, on the French-Genevan border, was the home of Voltaire (1694–1778) for the last twenty years of his life. Pushkin is alluding here to Voltaire's satirical fantasy-novel *Candide*, in which, in the person of Candide's tutor Pangloss, he ridicules a popularized version of the optimistic philosophy of Leibniz (1646–1716), according to which "all is for the best in the best of all possible worlds"(which is the one in which we live).

p. 217, *magnetism*: The German physician Franz Anton Mesmer (1734–1815) (whose name gave us the word "mesmerize") developed a theory of "animal magnetism", according to which patients' disorders could be treated by the inducing of trances. Although Mesmer's theory of "magnetism" was soon discredited, his techniques of trance inducement led to the modern practice of hypnotism.

p. 217, *they prophesy, and publish journals*: The references here are probably to the religious mystics, prominent in St Petersburg and at Alexander I's court during the latter part of his reign; one member of this group was the freemason Alexándr Fyódorovich Labzin (1776–1825), who was publishing a journal *Siónsky Véstnik* ("*Messenger of Zion*") at the time Pushkin was writing.